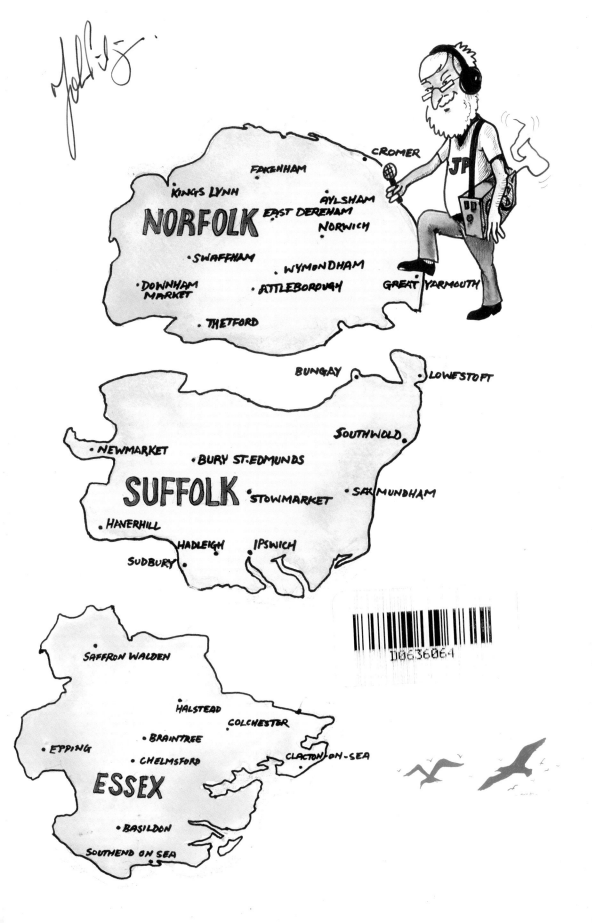

"OUT AND ABOUT AGAIN"

WITH

JOHN PILGRIM

WRITTEN BY JOHN PILGRIM

PHOTOGRAPHY BY DAVID SPAIN

CARTOONS BY NICK MILSTEAD

PRINTED AND PUBLISHED IN 2000
BY ALPINE PRESS

ALPINE PRESS LIMITED
STATION ROAD
KINGS LANGLEY
HERTFORDSHIRE
WD4 8LF

TEL: 01923 269777

ISBN: 0-9528631-3-8

ACKNOWLEDGMENTS

It would simply not be possible to put a book such as this together without the knowledge and assistance of local history societies and museums. I am always pleased to interview local authors and others who have contributed to the enrichment of knowledge in their local area. Similarly tourist boards and individual establishments have been most helpful with the compilation of 'Out and About Again with John Pilgrim' my thanks to all of them.

THANKS TO:

Ernie Almond, Hazel Acus, James Allan, Sarah and Michael Betts (for the loan of their children Sam and Joe), Louise Bolwell, Battersea Dogs Home, Roy in Bletchley, Biggleswade History Society, Jackie Butchart, Sue Scott, Dave Cady, Jackie Clements, Vivienne Evans, East Herts Flying School, Fred in Luton, Gordon in Stevenage, Jinner Greenwood, Alan Holzer, Peter Houldcroft, Chris Hargeaves, Adelaide Johnson, Ted Mc Cormack, George Pilgrim, Bill Pilgrim, June O'Mahoney, Jon Richardson (Kodak Ltd), David Keen of The Royal Airforce Museum Hendon, Linda Seeley, Sue Scott, Pete Smith, Andrew Smith, Brian Saunders, Cliff and Olive Smith, Natalie Tkachuk for the Benny Green photo, Bernard West, Bryen Wood of Bushey Museum, Dawn Tebbutt, Ron Thomson, Cuffley Camp, Knebworth House, Bernard West, Scott's Grotto, Roys of Wroxham, George Piggin of Chesham, Dacorum Heritage Trust, Vicky Nunn, Edwina Currie MP, Roy and Esme Brigginshaw, Henry Moore Foundation, The Old Palace - Hatfield House, Ashridge College.

We would like to thank David's photographic assistant Natalie Tkachuk for her help in the production of this book, Roy Williams for the use of his paintings and Nigel Gayler (Producer).

Special thanks to Mark Norman, Manager of BBC Three Counties Radio

KODAK LTD.

We would like to acknowledge the support given by Kodak Ltd in supplying all the photo materials necessary for the production of this book

George Eastman (1854 - 1932) invented the Kodak roll film camera and developed the process for making dry photographic plates in 1880. He subsequently pioneered the use of transparent photographic film. The first Kodak camera was marketed in 1888 and Kodak also offered a developing and printing service. Eastman gave half his fortune to educational beneficiaries. In the UK from their Hemel Hempstead offices Kodak have become very much part of the local community.

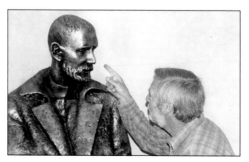

George Eastman (1854 - 1932)

INTRODUCTION

"*Write another one*" they said, and I agreed, but everything has its downside, for a start it meant that I had to spend some more time with David Spain! If you read the first '*Out and About*' book you will know that David is a somewhat overweight ex-public schoolboy photographer (by that I mean he attended a public school and now takes photographs, not someone who takes photographs of ex-public school boys). Still '*Spainy*' does take the occasional '*snapshot*' as you will see as you leaf through the pages on this tome. You will also notice that I allude to the various places that the Pilgrim family have called home over the years, we have moved house on several occasions and each time we have attempted to put down our roots, the wanderlust has taken over. Sometimes it has been because I wanted to change career and sometimes simply because the dustbin was full! It has never been because, (as my friend Ernie Almond would have you believe) the locals had all heard my jokes. Ernie Almond you will hear more of a little later, for now let me explain that you will (hopefully) learn something of the several counties the Pilgrim tribe has lived in, worked in and loved for various reasons. All of the characters you will hear about (well nearly all) do or did exist, most of them I have been happy to call '*friend*' and none of them owe me money, nor I them!
So read on and enjoy.

John Pilgrim, Sandy, Bedfordshire

August 2000

TABLE OF CONTENTS

TABLE OF CONTENTS

MY FAMILY AND OTHER PLACES
NORFOLK · MUNDESLEY · SHERINGHAM · THE BROADS

We lived in Norfolk for over seven years so I thought I knew what to expect when I suggested to my wife that it would be fun to take our two grandsons for a 'bucket and spade' holiday. Naturally I hadn't considered the fact that since their mother (our daughter) was now thirty two years old, her parents (that's us) are getting on a bit to take a three and five year old away for a week. The first thing we got wrong was packing the car, normally this involves stuffing our belongings into a couple of cases, adding my tape recorder and note books and off we jolly well go. This time we packed our cases and then Sarah arrived with the boys, but not just with the boys, with their luggage for a week in Norfolk by the seaside!

Norfolk Broads, 1969

So we tried three different ways of loading the car and then decided to:

a) load the boot, b) load the boys and c) pack everything that was left over around the boys. This worked quite well and we left on time. The boys behaved themselves extremely well on the two hour journey, this was mainly due to the fact that Auntie Emma (our middle daughter) had supplied us with a box of sweets, the contents were liberally sprinkled onto the back seat of the car each time either Joe or Sam uttered the immortal phrase. "Granddad/grandma I love you".

We took a very direct route, the A1 north and then across country avoiding towns like Huntingdon and Wisbech. I'm not a great admirer of Fenland, I find it too flat and treeless, the towns and villages look as if they require a face lift and where a new house has been built it looks out of place. Planners over the past few years have been obsessed with modern building techniques and materials and houses look exactly the same wherever you go. Why can't they allow some more leeway to architects or why can't architects use a bit more grey matter? Beyond Wisbech and into Norfolk the countryside begins to get more interesting, and when you reach the boundaries of the Queen's Estate at Sandringham the properties start to look more cared for. I've never visited Sandringham, in fact I don't recall visiting any of the Royal houses, homes, stables, clock towers etc. I am fascinated by the history of Britain in general terms and therefore have to acknowledge the involvement of Royalty in our past but I much prefer finding out about what I call real people. Anyway, though the boys had been well behaved, they did begin to get a little restless as we neared our destination. It was at this moment that granddad made a crucial error! I pretended that we would not see any caravans on the road (of course I knew that we would but I thought it would serve as a useful diversion for the boys) so then I proceeded to compound the felony by offering a fee of five pence (per grandson) for each caravan they spotted. By the time Sammy and Joe's combined holiday account had reached the dizzy heights of seven pounds fifty pence granddad decided to re-negotiate the deal. As grandma shovelled sweets into their sweaty little palms I suggested that we should only count caravans being towed by cars, looking like demented gerbils with confectionery stuffed cheeks the boys happily agreed. Twelve pounds seventy five pence (per grandson) later we drove into Mundesley.

I have always been a sucker for a special offer at the supermarket and I pride myself that I can 'do a deal' with the best of them but as we pulled up outside the building that was to be our holiday abode for seven days I admit that I had second thoughts. True the road in which our house stood seemed pretty well maintained as did the dwellings that stood either side of our holiday 'cottage' but, our particular dwelling did appear just a shade derelict. The plastic down pipes had become detached from their clips and would serve no useful purpose in the event of a cloudburst, but that didn't matter did it? after all it was not going to rain. The paint (what there was of it) was peeling away from the timber (what there was of it) and the garden (what there was of it) was, to say the least, overgrown. Still outward appearances aren't everything are they? and one shouldn't judge a book by its cover should one? In this case one most definitely should !

As we entered the hallway (having squeezed through a small porch a foot high with free newspapers and local village magazines) it did occur to me that this was one deal too far and that divorce could well be imminent. I wasn't too worried about the boys, after all they were young and excited and were clearly of the opinion that anyone potty enough to shell out cash just for counting caravans would be a soft touch when it came to ice cream, amusement arcades and other exotic items available at a seaside resort. Oh no! it wasn't the boys who worried me, it was she who was at that very moment standing in the hallway staring with a look of disbelief at our 'cottage'. As Sammy and Joe began to explore the ground floor of number forty two, my wife of over thirty summers (or so) slowly lowered a rucksack (property of Sammy and containing various holiday necessities such as a kite, a batman outfit and a plastic monster) to the floor. Just in case you happen to be of the male gender, and have not been married, I would like to point out to you a couple of danger signals you may wish to bear in mind if you should decide to take the plunge. When a wife lowers a grandchild's rucksack to the floor, gazes around her with a 'dead behind the eyes' look and curls her lip, you are, in fact in some trouble. When she then takes a couple of paces into the house you have borrowed through a "friend of a friend" and makes for the kitchen, well the best thing you can do is unload the gear from the car as quickly as possible, engage both grandsons in this chore and do your very best to make them incredibly excited about their holiday, make plans with them very loudly, say things like "This afternoon we are going to build the biggest sandcastle Mundesley has ever seen", follow this statement with offers of large amounts of cash to be made available at all times and you might just get away with it.

Joe waiting for the bricks to turn up!

Sammy waiting to carry the bricks!

Grandad hoping the bricks don't turn up!

I did get away with it thanks mainly to the fact that we needed a holiday and the obvious problem that we should not disappoint the boys. The house was a cross between Hitler's wartime bunker and a junk yard. The "friend of a friend" who owned the place was clearly some sort of a nut who would collect just about anything as long as it was of no value at all and would gather dust. We settled in and I took a trip around the house. There was one really interesting room situated on the third floor, on entering I saw a double bed and a wardrobe of sorts and thousands of magazines! They were not strewn about the place but stacked in neat piles across the floor and quite obviously in some sort of subject matter order. I'm not really into steam railways, old cinemas or antiques so I only made a superficial inspection, but it was a good thing that I did notice a rather large collection of men's magazines! An hour later I heard the dulcet tones of 'Mrs P' drifting up the stairs and I hastily replaced a copy of 'Readers Wives' that I happened to be censoring back onto the pile - this was clearly a room the boys (or my wife) should not discover.

Mundesley is a hotch potch of fairly modern houses and Victorian buildings perched on the cliff top. Some of the buildings have a certain faded charm and the village centre, set back from the cliffs is quite pleasant. There is a Tourist Office and the lady who runs it was helpful. In truth you have to 'make' a holiday in Mundesley because the holiday will not come to you. Once you have made your way to the beach down a somewhat tortuous winding path you can hire a deck-chair and make sandcastles and chase the waves to your heart's content. The husband and wife team who were running the beach café and shop were most charming and their tea was just like mum used to make, though I doubt if they will be in residence when you visit, seaside business's being what they are, as precarious as some of the cliffs! In order to 'make' a holiday at such a venue you will require copious leaflets and our holiday 'cottage' had these in abundance. Shopping in Mundesley is restricted, there is a small supermarket for the day to day requirements of a granddad and grandma who have two small boys in tow. You can pay exorbitant prices for plastic sunglasses, kites, buckets and spades, baseball caps etc. at one or two cliff top shops. My advice to you is; "Get Out and About" - visit Sheringham Steam Railway for a start. It's pricey but well worth the trip. Sheringham is situated a few miles north of Mundesley and is a pleasant enough town. On the day we visited the wind was rapidly approaching gale force and we retired for a brief moment into a small restaurant to purchase ice creams, coffee and other sticky oddments beloved by grandchildren everywhere. I had whetted the kids appetite for the railway by explaining that we were going to see Thomas the Tank Engines' relatives, I'm no fool, I knew that Sam and Joe were besotted by Thomas and it was my way of getting them interested in the real thing. As I said the price of a ticket is a bit steep for a whole family but you really should take the trip. For my part I sank into my 1940s train seat and imagined that Jenny Agutter (you may remember her in the film The Railway Children) was about to appear on the line waving her undergarments. As it happened Ms Agutter didn't appear but the train rolled and chugged along a coastal route at a leisurely speed and we had a half hour stop at the turn around point, time enough for more ice cream which Joe managed to spread liberally over his face, down the front of his jacket and across the back of Sam's jumper as well'.

Having experienced the wonder of a steam train journey the boys were intent on taking a swim. The aforementioned gale had now reached typhoon proportions so grandma and granddad needed to make a decision, well in truth it was grandma (isn't it always thus) who decided. I entered Woolworth's, and for the princely sum of five pounds and fifty pence became the proud owner of a new pair of bathing trunks. I'm not mad on swimming but somebody had to do it and clearly Mrs P wasn't going to be the one. We made our way to the indoor pool situated just outside the main shopping area. By now the rain was slanting down and we dashed into the foyer to pay our money, granny (by now I had resorted to this description in order to get my own back) went to take her seat poolside while I changed into my 'Woolies' swimwear. Over an hour later I emerged from the pool somewhat wrinkled but elated (I went into the pool wrinkled but not in the same places), the boys thoroughly enjoyed making me sit on the fountains of water and Joe displayed amazing courage jumping into the pool with great whoops of joy. Money well spent and grandma placated granddad by allowing him to buy a fish and chip supper for all of us to eat in front of the television. So these modern, new fangled water pursuit centres do have a use after all.

So what of Mundesley itself? I hear you ask (or at least you should, do try to keep up) William Cowper the poet spent his final years on earth in this Norfolk village, to be precise he chopped and changed between Mundesley and East Dereham, don't ask me why because I don't know, he was suffering from depression at the time and claimed that the east wind got him down and finally left Mundesley altogether. In the Domesday Book the town is called Mulesai and made its living from fishing. The tourists came with the railway in 1898 and despite the fact that the railway has been defunct since 1964 they still come, not in massive numbers you understand but they can be seen flitting from one tea shop to another or gazing into the 'eight til late' store to decide which video to rent. Staff at The Royal Hotel will tell you that Horatio Nelson stayed there and in all probability he did, after all, he was born on the east coast. Inevitably on this coast you will always find a shipwreck story and Mundesley is no exception. On November 17th 1868, under cox William Withers, the lifeboat saved six men from one ship and the following day the entire crew of another. All Saints Church has been renovated over the years and is not particularly good to look at but it has its fair share of characters laid at rest in the churchyard. In Tudor times one of the rectors was a part time poacher and another, James Mitchell was a minor criminal, often in court.

So it's worth a visit is Mundesley but I do advise that you check out your accommodation more thoroughly than I did! Unless of course you fancy spending a week reading men's magazines while perched on a World War Two radio transmitter.

'The World's Largest Village Store'

Take a trip on the Broads, you know it makes sense! and on the subject of sense. When you visit the Broads and you have two small boys with you, do try to stay away from the shopping area in Wroxham. If you don't you will find that a visit to Macdonald's is required at least every two hours or so. Seriously though, Wroxham is a must for someone like me, not for the fact that it is very much the tourist centre for the area, but for ROYS OF WROXHAM!

It's billed as the 'World's Largest Village Store' and who am I to argue? It isn't simply the amount of shops involved with Mr Roy's business, nor the amazing range of goods, it's the story behind Roys that intrigues me.

Alfred Roy was born in 1838, he kept a shop at Reepham where he was also the village carpenter, he had four children and it was Alfred's son Arnold who was destined to become an extraordinary businessman. It is said that at the age of fourteen Arnold was given a donkey that no other person could handle, with a fortitude soon to become apparent the length and breadth of the county, young Arnold used the animal to tow a small soapbox barrow to the surrounding villages selling various items from his father's shop. The young man went to London and tried his hand at several jobs but he always felt the draw of the retail trade. On one occasion, when he was minding some horses to earn a few extra coppers, he made himself a promise - to set up something that would rival the big stores in London. The year 1895 saw our hero back in Norfolk, he persuaded his father to loan him some money and purchased a store in the village of Coltishall, brother (Alfred junior) returned to the county and together the boys (with the help of their family) became shopkeepers. Several astute business moves followed until they set up in Hoveton. The railway station was in Wroxham and the brother's supplies came addressed to 'Roy Brothers LNER, Wroxham' telegrams came to 'Roy Brothers, Wroxham', the name stuck and today holidaymakers from all over the world visit Roys of Wroxham, in Hoveton! Naturally the tourist business from the Norfolk Broads must be a mainstay of the business today. It is interesting to reflect that when the Roy family made their initial entrepreneurial moves, very few people could have foreseen the incredible success story. Today Roys of Wroxham is Wroxham, (well Hoveton actually).

Roys modern store at Wroxham

PLACES TO VISIT IN NORFOLK

North Norfolk Railway, Sheringham. Enjoy a trip on this well organised railway, there's a restaurant if you fancy something to eat and drink. Telephone the railway on 01263 822045.

Blakeney Point, one of the country's best areas for bird spotting and taking a look at the grey seals. Telephone the Warden's Office on 01263 740480

The Norfolk Broads, six rivers and about sixty broads to discover. The Broads were formed when locals dug peat for fuel in medieval times. Telephone The Broads Authority for more details on 01623 782281

Norfolk is well known for its windmills (I met my wife in a windmill, we've been going around together ever since!) The best place to find information is the Norfolk Windmill's Trust, Telephone: 012603 223219

Blickling Hall, Anne Boleyn lived in the original house, Henry's wives seem to have got about a bit, almost everywhere you go you can find a house where one of them once lived, but come to think of it old Henry got around a bit as well (perhaps that should read, put it around a bit!) Locals will tell you that on the anniversary of her death Anne turns up at Blickling in a coach, carrying her head on her lap. Telephone: 01263 733084 for details.

SUFFOLK -'BLACK SHUCK' - THE BATTLES OF SOLE BAY AND SAXMUNDHAM

We lived in Suffolk for several years, our three daughters were born in the county and grew up within a stone's throw of the seaside. Christmas Day was the time to take the dog (and the kids) for a stroll along the beach at Southwold. I make no apology for stating that Southwold is one of the real gems of the east coast. Formerly known as Swole or Southole, the town's only industry was curing sprats, these days tourism has to be the main source of income. Even on a wet and windy, and this part of the coast is normally windy, Sunday afternoon in midwinter Gun Hill is worth the visit. Here you can see several cannons facing out to sea and read, on the wall of what I think used to be a lookout point, about the battle of Sole Bay. In 1672 the Dutch attempted to repeat an earlier naval triumph (they had blockaded London for a time but finally had to retreat) by having a go at our fleet anchored off Sole Bay. High Admiral of the Fleet, James, Duke of York had set up his headquarters in Southwold and, somewhat uneasily the French had joined him. The British had but two hours warning of the Dutch attack and the French, (being French), immediately moved their ships out of harms way leaving the Duke of York to grab his sailors from the hostelries of the town. The Dutch were extremely well equipped and a bloody sea battle took place. The Duke's cousin, the Earl of Sandwich went down with his ship when it exploded, his body being washed up some days later on the shore and only identifiable from the star he carried on his charred uniform. Both sides claimed the engagement as a victory but stalemate was the real outcome, and the Dutch returned to Holland to polish their clogs and drink copius amounts of that egg drink we only buy at Christmas!

Gun Hill, Southwold

The Lighthouse at Southwold

The only place we could afford!

Spainy couldn't even afford these!

Many a happy hour was spent here

Southwold from the harbour

The open greens of Southwold were introduced in 1659 following a fire and they give the visitor the opportunity to wander freely. St. Edmunds church is worth a visit, overlooking the font is a Jack-o'-the Clock wearing the armour of the White Rose of York. Cafe's, restaurant's and bistro's abound and of course the local brewery is Adnams who use *'Southwold Jack'* as their emblem. Once you have taken in the fine cliff top views and observed the beauty of some of the fine Regency houses, take stroll to the harbour. As you make your way through the grassy dunes you will spy the somewhat ramshackle holiday homes of lesser mortals, for Southwold is not simply the preserve of the well to do. From the harbour it is possible, by means of the bridge to walk into Walberswick where the beach is sandy and the sea has made considerable inroads and there is an air of Dickensian England, in fact the great man is said to have stayed in the area. From Walberswick you can walk to Dunwich a place with a great history. In the days of Egric and Sigebert (wonderful names!) Dunwich had precedence over all other kingdoms of East Anglia and it flourished. In 1208 (that's a year not a time on your digital watch) King John granted a charter for which Dunwich was asked to pay 200 marks, 10 falcons and 5 gerfalcons (don't ask what a gerfalcon is, I haven't a clue). For rights over all wrecks on Dunwich shore the town paid the Crown five thousands eels annually. Catching eels is still practised, it seems that it is called *'pitching'*. To partake of this somewhat, in my opinion, overrated pastime, you will need to tramp through the bottom of muddy ditches seeking the eel blow-holes, there will be two spaced apart, in between the space lies your eel, now jab your pitch or spear several times into the mud until an eel is dragged out, at this moment you might like to reconsider your position, because the said eel will be writhing and lashing and covered in slime. If you find yourself *'ead over eels'* in love with this wild part of Suffolk I will not be surprised!

ANOTHER (MORE RECENT) BATTLE

The battle of Sole Bay in 1672 was, as we have learned, a bloody sea battle. In the year of our Lord 1970 another battle took place in the county of Suffolk, this time a few miles inland at the town of Saxmundham. Only twenty five men were involved and they all lived to tell the tale. It was Boxing Day and eleven men of Halesworth boarded a coach owned by Fosdike's Coaches and driven by one Rodney Fosdike (remember the name Fosdike it is central to the plot). They arrived in Saxmundham at 10a.m. after the overnight frost had 'firmed' the football pitch and the match referee, (a certain 'Nollie' Rankin) declared it fit for play. The first forty five minutes of the game gave no indication of what would happen in the second half and Saxmundham and Halesworth were happy with the interval score of one apiece. At the break the Halesworth captain, known throughout the Ipswich and District League as 'crunch Pilgrim' chatted with his friend and left back, 'Jinner' Greenwood, the pair agreed that the opposition centre forward (name unknown, parentage uncertain) would "have to watch it or he would find himself in trouble". The second half began quietly enough, 'Crunch' verbally driving his troops forward, 'Jinner' offering technical advice and Peter 'Slosh' Etheridge running rings around the opposition with skills honed over forty years or more. It had to happen of course, the opposing centre forward clattered into 'Slosh' leaving him in a muddy heap. There was no trainer but Tim Sherwood our linesman entered the fray with a bucket and sponge. Gently wiping the blood from 'Slosh's' hand Tim enquired "how do you feel now boy?" "Well my hand is clean but it's my ear that's bleeding" our hero replied. Mr Sherwood explained that he knew nothing about ears and suggested 'Slosh' should retire from action. Two minutes later the opportunity for revenge occurred when Saxmundham mounted a full frontal attack on the Halesworth goal, the ball landed at the feet of their centre forward, 'Crunch' arrived from the right and 'Jinner', always the master of the pincer movement came in from the left. The ensuing fist fight proved to be beyond the control of 'Nollie' who ran swiftly to Mr Fosdike's coach, as he mounted the running board he blew the final whistle. Egged on by the spectators (four from Saxmundham and the Halesworth linesman), the two teams continued the battle all the way to the changing room (for changing room, read converted chicken shed only recently vacated by the chickens). There being no facility to wash (or indeed time), the Halesworth men made their way to Fosdike's bus, whereupon Rodney announced that we would have to 'give him a push' because the bus was stuck in the mud. A rearguard action was fought by the Halesworth forward line while the defence pushed the bus out of the mire.

Oh yes! Believe me, when the youth of today talk about football, they know nothing! The Battle of Saxmundham was reported in detail by the Halesworth Times and the story is still talked about today in the bar of The Halesworth Labour Club. The above is a true and undeniable account of what happened, at least in Halesworth it is!

ON THE SUBJECT OF HALESWORTH

When I last visited Southwold, I purchased a book about Suffolk and turned immediately to the page on Halesworth. The author dismissed the town where my daughters were born in just a few lines, what a cheek! Halesworth is a friendly, pleasant town with its own place in history. Quite apart from the fact that we once lived there, Halesworth (in times past) had its own currency, not that I saw much of any type of currency when we lived there. We had only been married for about a year and money was a bit tight. We made some great friends though, people who have remained friends for over thirty years. 'Jinner' Greenwood was built like the proverbial outside toilet (I can't use the exact phrase here, but you get my drift!) I first met 'Jinner' at a football training session for Halesworth Town. I felt like a complete outsider and, looking back I suppose it was quite brave to join a village football team without knowing anyone (I was like that in those days, young and foolish). As we laced our boots in the unheated changing room the club captain introduced me to the other lads, *"And this is Jinner, he lives in the same road as you"* he informed me, I smiled at the barrel chested, red haired apparition. 'Jinner' didn't look up, he simply muttered *"All right boy"*. Over the next few years 'Jinner' Greenwood and I spent many happy hours together. We rolled up our sleeves and fought to the death every Saturday afternoon for Halesworth Town Football Club, during the week we *'trained'* at the White Hart in Halesworth, we downed pint after pint of *'Sludge Water'* and Whitbread Tankard and heaved hay bales onto tractor trailers during the Summer months. 'Jinner' Greenwood is a Suffolk man through and through and I am proud to call him my friend. On one occasion, after some extra *'training'* in the White Hart, I dropped 'Jinner' off at his house (just about four houses from my own, but I couldn't allow him to walk!) We had purchased fish and chips and I meandered up my own garden path to the dulcet tones of 'Jinner' (who had been locked out) explaining to his wife, *"I've bought you some cod and chips darling, let me in"* clearly there was no answer from his spouse, *"Come on my beauty let me in"* implored my friend, still no answer, *"Well alright then, have the fish and chips anyway"* 'Jinner' stuffed the late meal through the letter box! My everlasting claim to fame in Halesworth is that I was the only footballer ever to put 'Jinner' into hospital. I have told that he was built on the rugged side, in fact he was on the trawlers for some years, out of Lowestoft, so you can imagine just how tough my friend was. It was Saturday afternoon and we were playing against Wrentham, a long ball pierced our defence, I set off in chase, 'Jinner' set off in chase, the Wrentham centre forward (wisely) gave up the chase, 'Jinner' and I didn't realise that we were the only contestants for the ball, as the spectators placed their hands over their eyes 'Jinner' and *'Crunch'* converged on the ball. 'Jinner' ended up in the Norfolk and Norwich Hospital and I count myself lucky that my friend didn't bear a grudge! On another occasion, 'Jinner' and I also spent a pleasant couple of hours on the roof of my bungalow, well it was Christmas Eve and we were young and we had been to the White Hart and the TV aerial needed fixing and, well that's the way of things in Suffolk.

So much for the early years of our marriage (that's Margaret and me, not 'Jinner' and me!) Schoolteachers often take a lot of stick, not from me. During the early years of our marriage we had a piece of good luck. When 'Jinner' and I were playing football for Halesworth Town a certain Pat Dunn (vicar's son) introduced us to a certain Dave Williams (who wrote a dissertation in Sanskrit and Pali) who introduced us to a Laurie Shepherd. Laurie was proud of being Welsh, proud of being a teacher and proud of being married to Maureen. We had two children, a house and a mortgage at the time. After being introduced to Laurie, I went home to tell my wife that I had met this 'mad Welshman'. Laurie Shepherd was quite simply the nicest, most talented man I have ever met. He was born the son of a milkman in Porthcawl, Wales. Laurie attended art school and became a teacher, no child could have ever wished for more. When I met him, he was at the very beginning of a quest, a quest to teach children the glory of painting and art. Laurie introduced me to Alan Holzer a history teacher and so began

The Thoroughfare, the shop on the right used to be Vanstone's

one of the happiest periods of our life. Laurie and Alan were both married to girls named Maureen, and the six of us became lifelong friends. Extrovert Laurie and modest Alan and their wives were polls apart politically, they would argue for hours on end. Laurie would suggest 'Sending in a gunboat' to cure a political crisis, Alan would reasonably talk of mediation. Their wives would smile and leave them to it. Margaret and I would revel in our new found friendship. No two teachers could have offered more to their pupils. Alan taught history as it should be taught, Laurie taught art with passion. Alan Holzer was (and still is) involved in local politics. Laurie Shepherd sadly passed away in 1999. Laurie's funeral filled Halesworth church to overflowing, it closed the local school and brought home to the parents and children of Halesworth just how much a man can achieve.

As for the man who dismissed Halesworth in a few lines of his book, well hard luck sir, it is your loss.

In the 70's I believe Mrs Ives ran the shop on the left

'BLACK SHUCK' AND OTHER LEGENDS

In the area around Southwold, Halesworth and Bungay the tale is told of 'Black Shuck'. The town sign of Bungay shows the castle and a black dog stabbed by forked lightning, the dog is said to represent the Devil and has a strong resemblance to 'Black Shuck'. This creature is mentioned all over Suffolk but near the coast where we lived he is described as a hound from hell whose howling forecasts disaster. In Bungay they will tell you that 'Shuck' once rushed into the church in broad daylight and tore the throats of the worshipers gathered there. My friend Alan Holzer who lives in Halesworth and who knows about these things maintains that the 'Shuck' story was useful to local smugglers when they wanted to keep the local population off the streets. It would have been easy to string a lantern around the neck of a dog or a donkey and drive it through the unlit streets while the smugglers carried out their illegal trade. Mr Holzer being an historian and a good socialist decided to preserve the tradition in Halesworth by calling his large black dog 'Shuck'.

Ghost stories abound in this wonderful country of ours and almost every region has its fair share of 'ghostly hounds from hell'. East Anglia has more than its fair share of doggie tales and mostly 'Shuck' is the name used. It's derived from an Anglo-Saxon word for a demon or goblin. In an article I have seen, one M.W. Burgess reports over one hundred sightings of 'Shuck'. Burgess mentions the sighting in Bungay Church and is very specific, it happened on Sunday 4th August 1577, 'Shuck is said to have left the marks of his red hot claws scorched into the wood of the north door of the church, not content with that the hound is said to have visited Blythburgh Church on the same day. In 1974 a large white hound was seen by a woman in London Road Cemetery, Beccles, it just faded away as quickly as it appeared. Blythburgh seems to be a favourite spot for 'Shuck' and it is a wonderful place to visit, at least Blythburgh is a great place to visit provided you don't lose your outboard motor!

Blythburgh Church, 2000

Always Check Your Outboard Motor!

One of the many jobs I have had in my time, was as a House-master at a Home Office Approved School (David Spain's school was approved but not in the same way). By and large the young men who were placed at the school were decent lads who had, for one reason or another broken the law (there but for the grace of God go I). We tried our very best to arrange for the lads to spend some sort of a Summer holiday at home with their parents but there was always a group who had nowhere to go, it was this group who found themselves spending a couple of weeks with yours truly and a couple of colleagues.

I like to think that we did a good job and indeed some of the young men have appeared recently to tell me that they remember these trips with some affection. Because I knew Suffolk pretty well I suggested that we should take some tents to a camp site at Southwold. As was the custom we drew up a work rota, each day a member of staff and a group of boys would cook the main meal, another group would clean the tents out etc. As I recall, Dave Welch our Physical Education Instructor (I hate PE Instructors, they are so fit and full of themselves) suggested that we should take some canoes with us, what a fool he was! We put the canoes into the water at Southwold and the lads (accompanied by Mr Welch) set off to paddle inland to Blythburgh. I, meanwhile (no fool) followed in a small boat powered by an outboard motor, my crew consisted of a couple of the lads who didn't fancy paddling a canoe. All went well and we arrived at the pub opposite Blythburgh church at the agreed time. We ate our packed lunch and Dave Welch ordered 'his boys' back into their canoes. My crew plonked themselves into the 'support boat', we had only been going for a couple of minutes when the outboard motor was snagged by something in the water, a brief inspection revealed that we had lost our propeller! No problem we had a pair of oars, BUT! The sand flats around Blythburgh are tidal and the tide was on the wain (or the wax, what do I know, I'm not a sailor) and it was left to me to row us back to Southwold. I have no idea just how long it took but I do know that my crew was of no help at all. They spent the entire voyage moaning and groaning as I 'grounded' the boat, exhausted their entire cockney vocabulary while I tried to navigate the river and pointed out that it was their turn to cook the evening meal and couldn't I hurry up? We had to pay for the lost propeller, which, I found out later had been 'snagged' by local fish poachers nets. Such are my memories of Silly Suffolk.

PETE IN STOPSLEY (LUTON)

Pete Worby is a regular caller to the radio programme and one day we found we had Halesworth in common. Pete is a member of the 56th Fighter Group, Halesworth Memorial Association. The association invites you to take a look at their museum dedicated to the men who flew from Halesworth and the surrounding area in World War II. They are a hard working bunch and deserve your support. The museum is situated near the Bernard Matthews Turkey factory which lies between the A144 and the B1124 about two miles north east of Halesworth. The museum is open on Sunday from 2.30pm during the Summer, admission is free.

FRAMLINGHAM CASTLE - THE CENTRE OF POWER IN SUFFOLK

Framlingham Castle has thirteen towers and there are spectacular views over the town. The castle has been a fortress, an Elizabethan prison, a poor house and a school. Telephone: 01728 724189

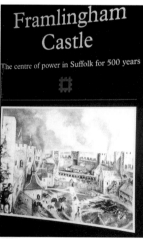

PLACES TO VISIT IN SUFFOLK.

Saxtead Green Post Mill ceased production in 1947 and you can still see the whole superstructure turn to face the wind, there's plenty to see in the way of old mill machinery as well. Telephone: 01728 685789

The National Horse Racing Museum in Newmarket will explain the relationship between people and horses over two thousand years. You don't have to be interested in horse racing, the museum exhibition shows how the horse has been used in agriculture, war, transport, literature and entertainment. Telephone: 01638 667333

The Museum of East Anglian Life is situated in seventy acres in the heart of Stowmarket, there's a play area for the kids and a café as well. Telephone 01449 612229

Somerleyton Hall is a Victorian stately home set in twelve acres of gardens with magnificent trees and shrubs, the Maze of Yew hedging is the highlight. There's a gift shop, tea room and picnic area and it's close to the seaside town of Lowestoft.
Telephone: 01502 730224

Kentwell Hall, Long Melford is a moated Tudor House. You can wander the gardens see the Carp filled moats, the working Ice House, the camera obscura and much more besides.
Telephone: 01787 310207

A Couple of Broadcasting Tips!

When you have been working in broadcasting for a while you enter a dangerous period, you begin to become blasé about the whole thing. If you have any sense this is the time you try to concentrate one hundred and ten percent. I was lucky enough to have a man working at the radio station who was able to see me through this period, his name is Jeff Winston. It was Mr Winston who gave me the opportunity to broadcast in the first place and it was he who, when I told him how many letters and telephone calls I had received following my first broadcast advised me, *"Do not let it seduce you, my boy"*. He was full of words of wisdom was Jeff and usually delivered those words in his own inimitable style. I had only known him a few weeks when he decided to tell me how to use laughter on the radio, climbing onto a chair and making his way around his office using his desk, filing cabinet and other chairs as stepping stones he explained *"Laughter is like salt and pepper, use them sparingly"*. Having completed a circuit of the room, he sat down at his desk and continued to work as if I wasn't there. Basically Jeff was right, you cannot afford to take anything for granted just because you have early success. One Saturday morning I had arranged to tape an interview with Edwina Currie, at the time Ms Currie was standing as a candidate in the European elections and, looking back she was only willing to talk to little old me because she would talk to anyone in the media. Still it made me feel important and I confess that the lady in question was most agreeable. I interviewed her for about twenty minutes on her favourite subject, herself! She explained how she went to school in Liverpool, was a friend of the Beatles, how she struggled in politics etc. When she left the studio I couldn't wait to listen to my interview, I rewound the tape and pressed *'play'* **NOTHING**, in my attempt to prove how professional I was I had failed to press the *'Record'* button! Since that time I check everything.

Edwina Currie, Liverpool schoolgirl before she had egg on her face!

I Shouldn't Be Telling You This

I can't tell you where it happened and maybe I shouldn't tell you at all, but I'm going to. Over the years I have organised many outside broadcasts and roadshows, mostly they have been hard work but fun. The team usually '*muck in*' helping to build the stage, set up the outside broadcast unit and generally do what is necessary to produce a live stage show as well as broadcast programmes on the radio. We take it in turns to pay exorbitant prices for bacon sandwiches and a plastic cup containing a tea bag and hot water from those stainless steel wagons which litter all show sites. I say we take it in turns, we did have the pleasure of Simon Lederman's company for two summers but I never did see the contents of his purse!(If you read the first '*Out and About*' book you may recall that Mr Lederman broke '*The Great Thrift*' record by travelling through the South of France for three days without putting his hand in his pocket!) However Simon was involved in rather a dirty trick I played on someone who was so full of his own importance it wasn't true. We had worked particularly hard at one show ground, regular inserts into radio programmes had been made throughout the day and we had encouraged people to visit the show, in addition we entertained the crowds with our '*Roadshow*'. Towards the end of the day I was talking to one of the team when a man walked up to us and said "*The Mayor will be ready in fifteen minutes*", I replied "*Well good for the Mayor*" and continued with my conversation. The stranger spoke again "*You don't seem to understand, the Mayor is always interviewed on your radio station at the end of the carnival day, he will be ready in fifteen minutes*". Now I quite like interviewing Mayor's, it's part of what I do but we had not been asked to make any arrangements and there was simply no way that I could butt into a live radio programme with an interview. The Mayors representative insisted the interview would go ahead and implied that '*heads would roll*' if we didn't comply.

I made my decision and called Simon Lederman over to the radio car, I handed Simon a pair of headphones and microphone and told him to sit in the car. "*What am I supposed to be doing?*" enquired my thrifty friend, "*In a few minutes the Mayor will turn up, I want you to sit him in the car beside you, twiddle a few knobs, stick the microphone under his nose and interview him*", "*But we have no live inserts arranged*", "*I know that, you know that, but his worship doesn't so just do it*". A pompous Mayor arrived, looked at us as if we were something the dog had left behind and was placed in the radio car for his interview, five minutes later he left without saying thank you and we returned to our work safe in the knowledge that we knew something he didn't! I live in hope that Mr Mayor asked his wife what she thought of his interview when he arrived home!

Pilgrim and Lederman

MORE TALES OF CROXLEY GREEN (HERTFORDSHIRE)

I still have no idea how my dad did it! I have checked with my brothers and sisters and they all say he did, he had a day job and a night job. Sometime after the war ended (I came along in 1942) A.G. Pilgrim ('AG' to his friends) took a job as Night Watchman with Lapointe Tools on Otterspool Way, Watford, well Bushey really I think, anyway it was a fair old cycle ride from Croxley Green. I know it was a long cycle ride because, on occasions my dad would forget to take his packed lunch with him and I had to deliver it to the factory. He knew that I would be coming because mum always telephoned ahead (yes we had a telephone, mainly so that dad could keep in touch with his bookmaker and my brothers could play Kay Starr records to their girlfriends down the line!) Anyway, I would arrive, usually after dark at the factory gates with the aforementioned lunch. I can't remember how I actually got into the factory, perhaps dad left a door open, but I do know that the lights would be out and the machines standing idle bathed in moonlight and, just as my tummy tightened with that enjoyable fear children enjoy when playing '*sardine*' or some other fanciful game, the factory intercom would crackle and dad's voice would echo through the factory "*calling all cars, calling all cars*" he would whisper in a ghostly voice. Don't ask me why my old man thought this was funny, I rather fancy that the phrase "*calling all cars*" was what the police used at the time, but I can look back now on a rather small but pleasant memory.

Back to 'AG' and his two jobs, having finished his stint as night-watchman he would cycle home, have some breakfast and then cycle off to '*Campions*'. He must have got some sleep during his '*night duties*' because 'Campions was the home of Doctor and Barbara Woodhouse and he would have had little time to rest working for them. You may recall the name Barbara Woodhouse, she was the lady who breathed up cows noses and taught dogs how to behave. I remember the lady as being rather frightening, but then I was young at the time. Mrs Woodhouse had great energy and was to be admired for the forceful manner in which she literally made herself famous. '*Campions*' stood (in fact still does) in the corner of the beautiful village green at Croxley. Across the road from the house the Woodhouses had some farm land where they kept a few cows. The farm was run by Mrs '*W*' and my dad. Doctor Woodhouse worked at a large London Hospital, they had three children who were looked after by '*nanny*' (this lady was very old and had cared for Mrs '*W*' in her youth). Despite my fear of his mum I did enjoy spending my Summer holidays with Patrick her youngest son, looking back they were wondrous days even if I did feel a bit like the '*poor man's son*' allowed to visit the '*Big House*'. I didn't enjoy cleaning out the prize bull's pen though, the massive animal would allow me into the pen and stand facing the wall munching his food, at just the right moment the devil would try to shift me with his bum so that I would be in the right position for him to butt me!

Mrs Woodhouse began writing books about her dogs, Juno and Jyntee who were Great Danes and there was a horrible little Chihuahua called Chico (I think). '*Busy Barbara*' wrote and self published the books and carried them in the boot of her car to book shops where she talked (boy could she talk) the owners into taking them to sell. She also made some films, children's stories really, about the adventures of the dogs. The films were made in and around the farm and my dad appeared in them as indeed he did the books. If anyone has a copy of '*Jyntee the Dog With A broken Tale*' or '*Juno, Daughter of Jyntee*' my dad is the man trying to break into the Woodhouse car and, is also the judge at a dog show!

The original 'Campions', Croxley Green, home to Barbara Woodhouse

Croxley Green Windmill circa 1900

The barn of 'Campions' house

The later 'Campions' of the Woodhouses

THE QUEEN CAMPS IT UP!

When Jackie Clements from Stopsley telephoned my programme in which I had asked listeners to talk to me about camping, it turned out that Jackie had knocked in the odd tent peg with the best of them. Back in 1961 Jackie and her family lived in a council house in London, the family had always had an interest in Guiding and Scouting and Jackie was invited to join a very special group of Girl Guides. It seems that Buckingham Palace had decided that a new troop should be formed and meetings would be held at the London home of none other than Princess Anne. Clearly this would be no ordinary gathering around the camp fire and Jackie explained how she and her friends were collected by a chauffeur driven car and taken to the Palace for weekly meetings. As they drove through the gates of the Palace, Jackie and her friends would wave at the groups of sightseers as they pretended to be visiting dignitaries. When David Spain (who is known to have flirted with the odd woggle himself when he was younger) visited Jackie at her home, she showed us her scrapbook of letters from the Palace, the whole thing seems to have been organised by a Lady in Waiting and each letter is signed in her own hand. Jackie remembers clearly being very impressed by the fact that Princess Anne was just *'one of the girls'*. The Guides were allowed to use the Royal swimming pool and Jackie described one of those old fashioned wooden sauna contraptions where you sat down with just your head poking out of the top, I can just visualise the Duke in that! Jackie says that, at the time she and her friends didn't really feel that they were taking part in anything very special, I suppose that at their age you wouldn't. Looking back on it now is a different matter though, for instance, at Christmas the Guides put on their own pantomime at the Palace. HRH Anne naturally played Cinderella and all the girls parents were invited. Mrs Clements bought a new pair of gloves, a hat and new shoes for the occasion (as, I have no doubt did Mrs Windsor) and had difficulty making a curtsey to the Queen while she was holding a cup of tea in one hand and a cake in the other. The Queen Mother spent a long time with Jackie's dad chatting about Scouting and young Jackie got a cuddle from Prince Charles! Well not so much a cuddle more of a squeeze really, she tripped as she was leaving the stage and Charlie grabbed her. Jackie also claims to have seen Prince Andrew naked! Well he was baby at the time and when you are a young guide wandering about the home of one of your friends I suppose that sort of thing happens.

AKA-BRADSKYWALKER

22

Jackie with letters from the Palace

Although Jackie has all the letters from the Palace and a copy of the panto programme the only photograph of the period is one from a national newspaper. It seems that the girls could take photographs but the rolls of film had to be sent off to the palace who removed all those which included the Princess before processing, this would be paid for by the Royal Household and the remaining photos returned to the girls. We did see a Christmas card from Anne to Jackie though.

JUST THINK!

There are some middle aged men out there somewhere who, to this day will never know just how close they once were to Royalty. The Guides went off to camp and the young Princess was allowed to join them, (true Anne went by private car to the site while the others made their own arrangements). On the second day at camp the girls all wandered off across the fields and came upon a site where, **WAIT FOR IT**! Boys were camping. The two groups chatted for a while and then went their separate ways. So if you were a scout in the sixties and you tried to chat up a Girl Guide who spoke rather well, displayed a working knowledge of Buckingham Palace or maybe invited you to '*naff off*' when you asked if you could take her home, that would have been her!

CARRY ON CAMPING

David Spain and I left Jackie's home in Stopsley and made our way across Luton to meet a man who can, in all honesty be called an anorak. Pete Smith has a passion for restoring old caravans, I don't mean ten year old caravans, I mean old caravans, like from the 1920s and 30s. The Historic Caravan Club was formed in 1993 and to date has around five hundred members, they are dedicated people who not only restore the caravans but really do use them for their holidays and weekends in the country.

Travelling showmen and later gypsies took to the road in all sorts of horse drawn caravans in the early 19th century, but it was one Dr W. Gordon Stable who, it is generally accepted came up with the forerunner to all those chrome covered beasts that drive you mad during the summer months on our roads. The 'Wanderer' was a custom built home on wheels, eighteen feet long, it was built by the Bristol Carriage Company and based on their Bible waggons of around 1880. Dr Stable sounds quite an interesting chap as it happens. He wrote story books for boys and used his caravan as a mobile study. I am told that Stable's most well known story is about an epic journey he made through Scotland and is entitled 'The Cruise of the Land Yacht Wanderer'. Other 'Gentleman Gypsies' followed the example of the good Doctor resulting in the formation of the original Caravan Club in 1907. You can see Stables 'Wanderer' at the Bristol Industrial Museum.

In 1919 manufacturers moved away from horse drawn caravans and really got their teeth into motor traction. The first Eccles trailer appeared in 1919 and a firm called Piggots, who made tents turned their hand to producing vehicles made with canvas and solid panels. Streamlined caravans came along in 1930 and, in the opinion of some caravan aficionados much of the exterior character and charm disappeared. I am informed that, during the pre war years caravanners were quite 'well off' and Lords, Earls, Majors etc. were well into the camping and caravanning scene.

Winchester 15 Touring Caravan, from 1933 showing interiors

When Pete Smith showed to David Spain and myself his caravans, all lovingly restored to their former glory the light shone in his eyes and he told tales of happy weekends cooking up a storm on the original oven, collecting water from the communal tap, lighting gas mantles and happy chats under the awning. Over the years Pete has met up with genuine travellers who spent their lives caravanning around the country and they, in turn have given him instructions as to how he might do things like cook a rabbit stew. It seems you start by placing the stew on the cooker (outside the caravan, to avoid too much smoke) at around 6 a.m. the stew becomes edible by 6 p.m.! - I bet Pete and his friends can also relate tales of a strange language often used by motorists who try to overtake them as they wend their way through the English countryside!

You can join Pete and his Historic Caravan Clubbers simply by making a telephone call: 01591 610336. NB You don't have to own a caravan to join.

DAYS WHEN THE EXCITEMENT WAS 'IN TENTS'

Cuffley Camp was *'the place'* when I was a kid, we all aspired to making a trip to the Hertfordshire camp site when it was our school's turn for a *'holiday'*, sadly I was never able to go, I don't know why, perhaps the thought of spending nights as well as days with the young Pilgrim was just too much for any teacher to imagine. As I sat day dreaming at my desk about Cuffley Camp, *'Spainy'* would have been off with his public school friends (all wearing shorts too long for them, if you know what I mean) making a proper tented village in the Swiss Alps, no doubt singing *'I Love To Go A Wandering'* and sporting the very latest in designer rucksacks.

Way back in the mists of time Cuffley was an area of natural mineral springs, Royal parties visited to take the waters. Evidence of the existence of the wells can be found in the names of some of the roads in the area, *'Kingswell Ride'* being just one, very few of the wells are visible these days but history has it that the area was a popular hunting ground for Royals. As with many other towns and villages Cuffley began to really flourish when the railway arrived, the Great Northern extended its line through to Hertford from Enfield and the Cuffley Viaduct was constructed. An incident during World War One happened in the skies above Cuffley, one Captain Leefe Robinson shot down a German Zeppelin Airship. It crashed into Plough Lane and caused quite a rumpus as sightseers gathered to collect a grisly memento or two, locals made brooches, fobs and other items from their *'pickings'*. I was rather pleased to glean this information because I had often wondered about a pub named *'The Leefe Robinson'* and never (until now) took the trouble to find out more. Evacuees from London came to Cuffley during World War Two and some locals still recall seeing these somewhat lonely children being shepherded around the village. It seems strange to visit Cuffley now and realise that it was seen as a safe haven during the War, after all London is only down the road.

Following a broadcast, when we talked about Leefe Robinson listener Dave Cady telephoned to tell me that Leefe Robinson died from influenza at the tragically young age of twenty one. It seems that the outbreak of 'flu between 1919 and 1921 accounted for more deaths than the Great War.

ZEPPELINS OVER ENGLAND

SUNDAY SEPTEMBER 3RD 1916, AT 11.30PM LT LEEFE ROBINSON VC TOOK OFF FROM SUTTONS FARM, HORNCHURCH (39SQN) IN A BE2C AIRCRAFT TO ENGAGE ENEMY ZEPPELINS, 16 OF WHICH TOOK OFF THAT NIGHT FROM BASES IN BELGIUM AND GERMANY. THE ZEPPELIN SL11 CROSSED THE COAST ABOUT 12 MIDNIGHT OFF SOUTHEND ESSEX ROUTED VIA COGGESHALL, BETWEEN CHELMSFORD, COLCHESTER AND SAFFRON WALDEN, PICKED UP GT NORTHERN RAILWAY AT ROYSTON ON TO HITCHIN AND OVER LUTON AT 1AM. AT LONDON COLNEY DROPPED 3 BOMBS, 2 MORE AT NORTH MIMMS AT 1.35AM, 2 MORE AT CLAYHILL, THEN INCENDIARIES AT COCKFOSTERS NEAR THE HOSPITAL. AT 1.45AM CROSSED THE GREAT NORTHERN RAILWAY LINE SOUTH OF HADLEY WOOD, THEN OVER SOUTHGATE TO WOOD GREEN AND SOUTH OF ALEXANDRA PALACE HORNSEY WHERE IT WAS PICKED UP BY SEARCHLIGHTS FROM FINSBURY PARK AND VICTORIA PARK. THE GUNS OPENED FIRE AND THE SL11 TURNED OVER TOTTENHAM THEN DROPPED 6 BOMBS AT EDMONTON AND 2 MORE AT PONDERS END, ALSO ENFIELD HIGHWAY AND FORTY HILL WHERE LT L ROBINSON PICKED UP THE SL11, AT ONE TIME HE HAD CLIMBED TO 12,900FT. HE DIVED ON IT 3 TIMES, RAKED THE HULL WITH INCENDIARY BULLETS AND IN SECONDS THE WHOLE AFT SECTION EXPLODED IN A SEA OF FLAMES. IT CRASHED AT 2.30AM, 1 ½ MILES NORTH OF POTTERS BAR AT CUFFLEY. 18 BODIES WERE RECOVERED FROM THE WRECKAGE, NEAR ST ANDREWS CHURCH AND CASTLE FARM. THE WHOLE LONDON WAS ILLUMINATED BY THE BLAZE. THERE IS A MEMORIAL STONE AT THE SITE ON THE RIDGEWAY, CUFFLEY.

THIS IS A PIECE OF WRECKAGE FROM THAT EVENT.

LENGTH - 649FT, DIA - 78FT, SPEED 63MPH

Photos top left, bottom left and right courtesy of Anthony Gregory

CUFFLEY CAMP - 'SPAINY' GETS STUCK IN A TREE

Cuffley Camp was, until 1811 part of an area known as Northaw Common, described as a large, trackless waste its history can be traced back to Norman times when it was owned originally by the Abbots of St Albans. The Abbots leased the land to the De Valoignes family for the princely sum of twenty five shillings and two hawks, later the land was restored to the Abbey until the crown took over in 1539. Elizabeth I granted the estate to Sir Ambrose Dudley, Earl of Warwick for thirty three pounds seven shillings and twopence - don't ask me how the good queen arrived at the price, or what the '*tuppence*' was for! From 1632 the land was owned successively by William Strode, Patrick Thompson and Lord Salisbury. In 1936 five hundred and fifty acres known as Northaw Great Wood was purchased by Hertfordshire County Council, and in 1938 the wood was first used by visitors and is now a National Park. Cuffley Camp, as we know it, was opened as the '*County Badge Camp*' in 1943 and in 1948 it became known as the County Schools Camp. Since those early days thousands of young children have visited, many of them experiencing for the first time the thrill of camping, but not me! Oh no, when Little Green Lane School took a week at Cuffley, I for some reason wasn't allowed to go. It's a shame I had to wait some forty eight years before taking in the delights of Cuffley because I am certain I would have joined in the singing around the camp fire with gusto (and if gusto wasn't there at the time, I would have enjoyed singing with someone else). Louise Bolwell showed '*Spainy*' and myself around and David became enraptured with the photographic possibilities. Many of the trees are very old and some have been pollarded giving a distinct Robin Hood feeling to the wood. I interviewed Louise beside a small stream, a fire was burning nearby and '*Spainy*' wandered off, we were well into our interview when we heard a plaintiff cry "*Do you think that you could help me*" my overweight friend enquired politely (David is always polite, they teach you polite at Merchant Taylors' School). For some reason best known to himself David had been overcome with the desire to squeeze himself into a hollow tree! Now I know that we had been romanticising about Robin Hood, Maid Marian, King Richard and all that stuff, but quite why '*Spainy*' thought he would be able to force his considerable bulk into a hollow tree is beyond me. Louise and I helped him out and brushing himself down he walked off muttering something about Friar Tuck.

AKA. BRAD SKYWALKER

KNEBWORTH HOUSE AND THE FEMININE INFLUENCE.

Knebworth House near Stevenage in Hertfordshire has quite a history and a great deal of it has been influenced by the ladies who have lived there. There have been Lyttons at Knebworth for over five hundred years, the present incumbent is David Lytton Cobbold second Lord Cobbold of Knebworth, now is that a grand title or what! David (yes we are on first name terms, do I mix in high society or not) is a smashing chap, always willing to come onto the radio programme and ever willing to discuss his future plans for Knebworth. It's a unique house thanks mainly to Edward Bulwer Lytton, David's great, great grandfather. Edward was an author, poet, dramatist and statesman. Charles Dickens was a frequent visitor to Knebworth and acted in 'Private Theatricals' at the house in 1850.

The Lytton family has a great tradition of battling for women's rights and it is one of the ladies of the house that I want to tell you about.......

Lady Constance Lytton was born in Vienna in 1869, she suffered for most of her life from rheumatic illnesses but this was not to hold her back in her fight for women's rights. After a formal education young Constance spent her early life at Knebworth where much work was taking place and one can only imagine that life was pretty good. Fraulein Oser came to Knebworth from Vienna to teach music and became a friend to Constance. Through various family circumstances Constance was called upon to assist her mother socially, a task she found somewhat dreary. In 1891 Robert, her father fell ill and died and Constance, now twenty two years old set out to comfort her mother. At this time Knebworth House was let and the family were unable to return there to live . For a while the family lived at various houses belonging to friends or family and it was in 1892 that Constance sailed for South Africa with her mother, in South Africa she met John Ponsonby and became friendly with him. This was a happy period in Constance's life and she fell in love with Ponsonby. After just three months in South Africa Constance and her mother returned home, but not to Knebworth, the family were short of money and Constance worked as a book reviewer and writer for a women's paper. Constance and Ponsonby maintained contact by letter and there were occasional visits when Ponsonby returned to England on leave. The way the story was related to me when I visited Knebworth, Constance would appear to have experienced some real '*highs and lows*' in her early life and there was plenty more ahead!

Constance became involved with the Suffragette movement and was imprisoned for her beliefs.

There is much to see and hear on a visit to Knebworth, the guides are well informed and friendly and make sure you visit the gardens as well as the house.

The formal gardens at Knebworth include a Gertrude Jekyl Garden, they were simplified by Lutyens in 1909.

Knebworth House stands in 250 acres of parkland, the kids will enjoy the Adventure Playground.

A hotel is situated adjacent to Knebworth, special rates are available for those attending weekend events at the house and park.

GOING UNDERGROUND WITH 'NUCLEAR BUNKERS' SMITH.

Andrew Smith is his real name but he is known as *'Nuclear Bunkers'* because of his fetish for *'Cold War'* missile silos and bunkers! This thirty two year old former Bank Clerk/ stand up comic/professional photographer and *'all round good egg'* contacted my programme when the subject turned to war time *'Pill Boxes'*. It seems that young Andrew became interested in things *'below earth'* when he was a lad travelling on the London Underground Well it kept him out of mischief I suppose. I got to meet Andrew face to face when we visited the Royston Cave (more of the cave later) and he seemed perfectly normal which was a bit of a surprise. Anyway, apart from exploring disused bunkers, (there are about two thousand in Britain according to *'Nuclear'*) Andrew has expanded his interest to caves and the odd grotto or three. He tells me that the bunkers on his list vary in size from small, three man affairs to long abandoned Regional Seats of Government which could have accommodated up to one hundred and fifty people on three or four underground floors. *'Nuclear'* seems to collect nicknames like he collects bunkers, his girlfriend *'Lolly'* calls him *'Mole'* (I assume that this is because of his hobby that we know about and not for some other interest which he would rather keep secret!) And so it was that D. Spain (who, with his public school background would probably have earmarked a place for himself in a nuclear bunker during the Cold War) and I (who naturally enough, as a mere grammar school lout would have been excluded) met Andrew in a small yard just off the main street in Royston, Hertfordshire....

JP with Peter Houldcroft and 'Bunkers' Smith

ROYSTON 'BOTTLE CAVE'

There is a sign on the wall of a building which directs you to the Royston Cave and it is true that the arrow points towards a small door in an alley but it is easy to miss. In 1742 workmen were renovating a building which had been used as a butter market, they discovered a mill stone set in the floor and, under the stone was the entrance to a cave that had probably been unused for some four hundred years. A small boy was sent down the shaft and one can only imagine what he must have thought when he reached the bottom. The chamber is seventeen feet in diameter (5.2m) and nearly twenty seven feet high (7.7m), roughly bell shaped it is decorated with low relief carvings. Thankfully (especially when you bear in mind the girth of David Spain), the chamber is, these days reached by means of a tunnel built in 1790 and leading the visitor under the main road. Many of the symbols and figures have now been identified and it is now known that a wooden platform once existed above the level of the carvings.

Much damage occurred over the years and in 1966 the Town Council installed new lighting and hand rails to make visitor access more amenable. Since then the cave has been administered by the Royston and District Local History Society, Peter Houldcroft published a pictorial guide to the cave through the society and it he who was our guide.

Peter Houldcroft is a wonderful guide, one of those people who is so clearly fascinated by history that he is able to pass on his excitement and knowledge in an understandable way. As David Spain's camera clicked away and *'Nuclear Bunkers'* Smith marvelled, Mr Houldcroft explained the history of the cave. It was once thought that the cave was associated with Lady Roisia (who gave the town of Royston its name), another theory was that it had been the home of a hermit or that it had mystical purposes. Peter told us that it is now accepted that the cave was the work of the Knights Templar, once a rich, influential and somewhat secretive organisation set up to assist and protect people visiting the Holy Places, the Templars fell into disrepute in the early 14th Century. Many members of the order were accused of heresy and tortured; the Order was suppressed by Pope Clement V in 1312. A number of the carvings in the Royston cave resemble those found in the Chatteaux de Chinon, France where it is known Templars were imprisoned, it is also known that the Order had properties in the Royston area. Peter Houldcroft's *'A Pictorial Guide to Royston Cave'* will fill in much more of the history surrounding this fascinating place, better still make a visit.

Views of Knights Templar carvings in the chalk walls

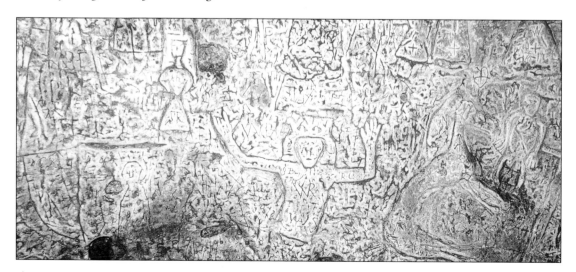

LIVE ON STAGE AT A THEATRE NEAR YOU!

John Pilgrim has convinced his radio colleagues Jon Gaunt and Ernie Almond to get 'Out and About' across Beds, Herts and Bucks. Your chance to see 'Gauntie' in the flesh! And maybe have a  drink and a chat before the show. This will be 'Gaunties' first  theatre tour for many years, John and Ernie look forward to getting in the odd word as well. It is a unique opportunity to meet, see and hear the Terrible Trio. Book early! Book Now!

"John Gaunt - Live & Unleashed!"

Where and When, The Number to Ring to Book Your Tickets.

Thursday   1st Feb. 2001 and Friday 2nd Feb. 2001 Luton Library Theatre - 01582 547474

Thursday   8th February 2001 Leighton Buzzard Theatre - 01525 378310

Saturday   24th February 2001 The Queen Mother Theatre, Hitchin - 01462 455166

Wednesday   7th March 2001 The Stables, Wavendon, Milton Keynes - 01908 280800

Thursday   15th March 2001 Corn Exchange, Bedford - 01234 269519

Friday   30th March 2001 The Alban Arena, St Albans - 01727 844488

To be arranged The Old Town Hall, Hemel Hempstead - 01442 228091

'Underground/Overground, the Wandering Three' (Nuclear Bunkers Smith, Spainy and Me)

Following our visit to the cave in Royston '*Spainy*' caught the underground bug. I tried to persuade him to take a trip on the Piccadilly Line but he was not to be put off, "*Find another cave*" he begged, so I did, well a grotto actually but it suited our purpose.

In a side street in Ware, Hertfordshire you will find Scott's Grotto an incredible monument to one John Scott, a Quaker businessman, poet and man of some vision. Scott moved to Hertfordshire when his father decided to remove his family from the dangers of disease ridden London. Mr Scott senior died in 1768 and his estate passed to John's protection. John's first marriage (in 1767) to Sarah Frogley, daughter of bricklayer from Hoddesdon, sadly ended when Sarah died a year later with their new-born child. In 1770 Scott married Maria de Horne, she was the daughter of a Quaker from Essex. Scott died in 1783 ironically of a fever in London where he had been sent for treatment. The family had never really paid much attention to Scott's poetical prowess or for that matter to his grotto building. Some time later Dr Johnson was asked to write about Scott's life, the venerable doctor replied "*as I have made some advances towards recovery*" (Johnson had been ill) "*and loved Mr Scott, I am willing to do justice to his memory*". Johnson died shortly after making this statement and it was left to a Mr John Hoole to produce the book on our hero's life. Scott's poems were also published up until around 1822, since then they have been ignored.In his guide to Scott's Grotto, David Pearman regrets the lack of interest in Scott's poetry thus. "*It is a pity for he was a gentle, charming poet*" I know little about poetry but I do know that John Scott left a wonderful fairytale grotto for us to visit.

Outside of Scott's Grotto, Ware, Herts

This is as close as we got!

It is said that the grotto took some thirty years to build and that work started in 1734 but since Scott would have been only four years old in that year I would suggest that the story is not accurate, I mean Scott was good but not that good! What seems far more likely is what John Scott told Mr Hoole, (you will recall that Hoole subsequently wrote Scott's story) "*In making the excavation under the hill, for the subterraneous passage*" Scott marched with his pick axe to "*Encourage his rustic assistants*", these assistants may well have been itinerant road builders for, it is said that Scott was responsible for the construction of the new Ware-Hertford Road. "*I have finished my Shell Temple*" Scott told another friend, Joseph Cockfield, this was in 1764 and he also requested that Cockfield should supply him with three or four hundredweight of melted glass or rockwork for the decorations inside the Grotto, shells were also collected by a Mr John Turner who was a nonconformist minister in Devon.

Grottos were very much the '*in thing*' during Scott's time but this fact alone is not likely to have been the reason for the construction. As a poet he may well have looked forward to a solitary place to write, and remember that the Scott family had a fear of living in London because of the disease in the capital. The grotto brought London society to Ware, Scott kept a visitors book and well over three thousand people '*signed in*', the aforementioned Dr. Johnson being just one such '*notable*'. '*There is simply no way that 'Spainy' could be seen as a 'notable*' (nor is it likely he could have signed his name in joined up writing) however my weighty photographic friend was as impressed as I and you will be as well.

Scott's Grotto is situated in Scott's Road close to the town centre for details of opening times telephone; 01920 464131.

WHERE? I MEAN WARE!

According to at least one archaeologist, Ware is probably one of the oldest occupied places in Europe, and if the High Street is anything to go by it has more cars per head than any city I know! Don't let the traffic put you off though, visit the Grotto and then take stroll around this pleasant Hertfordshire town.

Excavations have revealed settlements dating back to the Stone Age of some five to ten thousand years ago. One of England's oldest roads, Ermine Street crossed the river Lea at Ware. When the Romans arrived they widened the road for military purposes and the town grew up alongside the road. They found a *'slave shackle'* along with evidence of a possible *'slave export centre'* in the town, pleasant chaps the Romans.

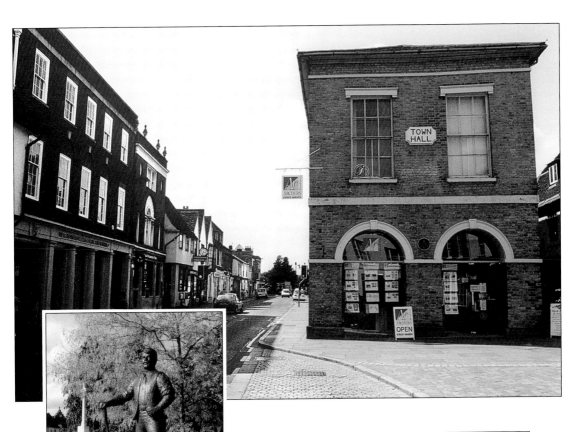

THE MALTMAKER
by Jill Tweed FRBS FRSA

unveiled on 4 November 1999
by Hugo Page Croft, Esq.

to commemorate the Millennium
and all the men who worked
in the Ware Malting Industry
from 1603 to 1994

Parlez Vous Francais?

It is part of the tradition on the 'Out and About' radio programme for me to greet certain listeners in French. Naturally I am fully conversant with the language, as indeed is Fred in Luton. When my screen tells me that Fred is on line twenty, I say "bonjour Frederika, petis pois?" and Fred replies in perfect French "Bonjour John, Edith Piaff et Rue de Remark". Other listeners often comment that Fred and I know nothing but this is simply not true, after all I am well aware that 'Pas de deux' is French for 'Father of twins' and that 'Coup de gras' means lawn mower. Similarly Fred (who once visited Calais for a day, asked for beret and came back with three pounds of sausages) will tell you that 'Piece de resistance' is a French virgin. Anyway notwithstanding other people's ignorance on the subject of La Belle France, let us tarry awhile in the land of Maurice Chevalier, (surely cheval means goat!).

'One Day, Maybe'

There's a house on a hill overlooking the Mediterranean Sea and I know exactly what it is like inside although I've never entered it. I know because it is my dream house, in a dream position. The main coastal road from St Raphael in the South of France to Monte Carlo runs past the door and one day it will be mine (the house not the road). In truth it is already mine because I have often gazed at it as I lay on the beach beside it, in my mind I have furnished it and re - designed the garden. There's a path leading directly down to where the sea laps onto the rocks (so I suppose it will have to be a rock garden) and I have even chosen the spot where my small, sea going - cruiser will be moored. In the afternoon, after a light lunch, my wife and I will take the cruiser over to St Tropez where we will dine at one of the hundreds of pavement restaurants. On Thursday evening we will stay overnight so that we can visit the street market in St Tropez on the Friday and perhaps have a cognac with Brigitte Bardot. This dream has some substance, we have often stayed in St Raphael (in my brother's flat) and we have smiled at Brigitte as she wandered through the Friday market (to date she hasn't smiled back), we have also paid something like seven pounds for a glass of cognac in 'St Trop' - just one of the drawbacks brought about by trying to live out your dream before you have the cash!
The house in question is just a couple of miles from St Raphael town centre, there is a small, rocky cove where we spend a great deal of time just reading and sipping white wine prior to a short dip in the warm sea. We have had many a barbecue in this cove, it is possible to set up your 'barbie' in the rocks and stand waist deep in the sea as you cook delicious sausages purchased at the local 'Leclerc' supermarket. During the course of the day a short, sun-tanned Frenchman visits the beach to sell small packets of peanuts, he is always most polite and I have even considered trying to muscle in on his business if it means that I could live all year round on the Cote D' Azur, 'Pilgrims Peanuts' has a certain ring to it don't you think? Situated half way down the slope leading to the beach is a small wooden hut where a large Frenchman with a grand moustache sells coffee and small cakes. His shack, for that is all it is, has two tables outside where you can sit to sip your coffee and listen to his family enjoying life in the tiny back yard hidden from the view of the customers - oh how I long to be one of the chosen few invited to join them! What a silly old sod! (me not the Frenchman with the large moustache) to believe that life could be so idyllic. Yet it is just possible that it could, I mean you could achieve your dream in one of two ways, either make a million quid a bit fast and move house or be a beach bum.

Being a beach bum is not as attractive as all that, one of the drawbacks would be living in an area surrounded by opulence. On visits to nearby Cannes I have witnessed the rich and beautiful (and the not so beautiful but rich) sipping their Camparis at pavement cafes while the traffic wardens attach parking tickets to their Mercedes, the parking problem is not cured by fines in Cannes because they can all afford to pay them. I have to say that watching the traffic wardens is quite fun though, they have uniforms designed by Christian Dior and figures to fill them!

No, the life of a beach bum is not for me, so it's back to blighty to purchase a couple of Lottery Tickets.

St Raphael - Frejus and St Tropez

You might like to know a little of the history of the area (no extra charge, but you could make a small voluntary donation to the John Pilgrim Cote D'Azur Settlement Fund if you feel inclined).

St Tropez: Began life as a small fishing village, the Greeks (from Marseille) established a port at St Trop (as we regular visitors call it) and the Saracens had a go at destroying it in 739. It was not an easy place to get to back then (and not too easy to reach now, in fact) being stuck out on a peninsula, but that is part of its charm. In the late 1800's the author Guy de Maupassant arrived (by boat) and proceeded to follow the somewhat novel lifestyle he had begun elsewhere, it is said that Guy went mad due to syphilis. A storm caused the ship of artist Paul Signac to put into St Tropez quite soon after De Maupassant's visit and he invited all manner of people to join him. Matisse, Dufy, Bonnard and Seurat took Paul's advice and St Tropez had something of a reputation by the outbreak of World War One. In 1956 something that was to prove exciting for me (a little later) happened - film maker Roger Vadim took Brigitte Bardot to St Tropez to film Et Dieu Crea la Femme ('*And God Created Woman*' to you and me). Hippies arrived in their droves in the '60s and the resort's place in history was sealed. Naturally I couldn't persuade David Spain to join me on my trip to St Tropez, he was much too busy in his dark room (and no doubt wondering exactly what '*Et Dieu Crea la Femme*' means), so it was left to me to take the photos.

St Raphael and Frejus: The Romans certainly knew how to look after their troops, St Raphael was a holiday resort for veterans of the Roman army. Frejus was a naval base for the troops of Julius Caesar and old Julius ensured that his boys had a good place to take a break. Following the battle of Actium in 31 AD the ships of Anthony and Cleopatra were sent to Frejus - you remember Anthony and Cleopatra don't you? They were the couple responsible for bringing Richard Burton and Elizabeth Taylor together, and I must say that Richard and Liz would have probably approved of this part of the Cote D'Azur today. The population of Frejus was greater in the first century AD than it is now, that is if you count only the main centre of the town. You can spend a rather pleasant day taking a look at the Roman remains of Frejus but you won't find much evidence in St Raphael, though there is still part of the aqueduct built by the Romans at the church, Eglise St-Piere, this brought water from Frejus to the church courtyard.

Photos of St. Raphael and Frejus, 2000

A Rather Different Trip to the South of France

I've told you before (and I promise I will tell you again) that all the really good stories on my radio programme come from the listeners. Ron Thomson lives in Sandy, Bedfordshire and he is a regular contributor with tales of World War Two. There simply isn't enough room here, to relate how Ron travelled by train through Canada and America (after an epic boat trip I might add), or just how he came to have a cup of coffee with Jimmy Durante in New York, or indeed how he met boxer Jack Dempsey. The list of well known people our Ron has met and chatted with is simply endless, so we will (with Ron's permission) leave those stories for another time. Instead I asked Ron to tell me about his visit to St Raphael in 1944.

"HMS Keren weighed anchor off Castelammare at midday Sunday, the 13th of August and, in line ahead with other ships, sailed across the Bay of Naples. Off Pozzuoli, a small port a few miles west of Naples where St. Paul had landed in 59AD, Keren swung westwards, took up her convoy position and headed into the Tyrrhenian Sea. The lower deck was cleared at 1600 hrs. and the crew mustered on the fo'c's'le to hear the Captain give a run down on what was happening. During the afternoon the Americans changed their dollars and lire into highly coloured occupational francs and drew rations of cigarettes, tobacco and candy bars. The soldiers and sailors whiled away their time swapping stories of the war and talking about family and loved ones. At 0600 hrs. the next morning, two hours before H-hour the coast could be seen, between 0700 hrs. and 0730 hrs. the ship was shaken by the bombs that were falling on the beaches eight miles away, individual explosions could not be heard - it was one continuous rumble. During the afternoon Allied bombers pounded the beaches - HMS Keren moved to within five miles of the coast, the reddish-brown mountains behind St. Raphael could be seen clearly and the Americans prepared to make their landing.

HMS Keren

RON TAKES UP THE STORY....

"*The Tannoy called the Americans to boat stations and they assembled in groups, the equipment was placed into the landing boats which were then lowered into the water. Many of the crew of Keren joined the Yanks on the boat deck to wish them well with 'sippers' of rum which they had saved from grog issue. The tension was eased and nerves calmed by superficial banter. "Hi Limey, if you ever get to Galva, Illinois look me up" - "When we've finished off Hitler I'm going AWOL in London to try some of your warm English beer, which is the best pub in Lie-cester Square?" - "Och don't ask me Yank, I belong to Glasgie".*

"Let's go C company - into the boats", Sergeant Galassi shepherded his group over the side, turned and shook hands with one of Keren's petty officers, "Thanks for the ride Limey" - "Best of luck Yank"

Sergeant Leonard Galassi turned to the ship's rail, crossed himself and climbed down the netting to join his buddies in the landing craft.

I never found out whether Sergeant Galassi came safely through those landings, I like to think he did. The German resistance at the time of the landings was concentrated on Red Beach where no Allied troops landed, instead they all landed without opposition at other points. In all 94,000 men went ashore with 11,000 vehicles in 1370 landing craft from 881 assault vessels on the first day. After the landings the Germans retreated along the Rhone valley leaving the Americans to enjoy a welcome from the French people that was so fantastic, that the operation became known as 'The Champagne Landing'.

Did Sergeant Galassi return to civvy street as I did? Did he marry and have kids? Is he, like me, being kept younger than his years by grandchildren? Do they ask him "What did you do in the war Grandpa?", and does he tell them about the time the British Navy took him and his pals to the South of France?

The people of Frejus and St. Raphael have erected memorials to those soldiers and sailors and airman who took part in the landings and I often pay them a visit when I'm in the area under much different circumstances to Ron. My thanks to him for his contribution both to this book and the radio programme.

With Yeoman Griggs at Port Tewfik

Ron at Port Said

BONJOUR TRISTESSE!

And so with the sounds of France ringing in our ears and dreams of returning some day with a bag full of money, it is time to gird our loins, pack our flip flops, sunhat, sunglasses, baggy khaki shorts and leather thong for we must board the train to Angleterre. Fred in Luton shares other memories with yours truly; as a child he visited the Essex seaside town of Jaywick. But just before we leave the South of France, observe the sunset over St. Tropez and imagine being a busker in such a place!

and so on to Angleterre........

JAYWICK

I can't say that I fell in love with Jaywick in Essex, nor that I particularly enjoy what it has become today, but it has its place in the Pilgrim family history. It was in the early nineteen fifties when Ivy Dorothy Pilgrim and Arthur George Pilgrim (my parents in case you wondered) embarked on a series of visits to the Essex resort. It was a special place in the sense that it provided us with the facilities to catch crabs (though in all honesty they were tiny, dirty looking things), paddle in the briny, race the waves to shore and use an *'Elsan chemical loo'*. One of the abiding memories I have of a week in Jaywick is the smell of the *'loo'* and of the noise (and the additional *'pong'*) when the man came to empty it! I also recall my father going missing shortly after our evening meal and my mum not wanting to tell me where he was. It turned out that he hadn't locked himself in our chemical closet for a bit of peace and quiet, but rather he had gone to join his mates at the illegal greyhound racing track. I'm not sure whether the track was really illegal but I am sure that *'betting'* would have been in those days. Depending on just how successful dad's evening at the track had been, he would return home with some *'goodies'* for us to enjoy, usually a packet of Smith's Crisps(the proper one's with a little blue bag of salt).

The first job each morning (apart from a visit to the *'Elsan'*) would be to take a walk along *'The Front'* as dad called it, to collect bread still warm from the oven. My memories of Jaywick are of the small things and all the better for that. I must have seen such people as *'Jimmy the Milk'* and Jim Shepherd because I know that such people are part of Jaywick folk lore.

I also know (now) that there were terrible floods in the area in 1953, Mary Lyons in her excellent book, *'The Story of Jaywick Sands Estate'* describes the floods and indeed the history of Jaywick through the ages. The floods devastated the area and the fight to save life and limb found heroes and heroines in unlikely guises. As the sea savagely sought to claim the land and the possessions of the residents, they fought back. A Jaywick business man and one time magician by the name of Smith owned a couple of pleasure dingies, he hauled these into action and together with his boatman Jim Smith worked for three days and three nights rescuing people. Elizabeth Allard, known as *'the little Florence Nightingale'* because of her work with the Jaywick Red Cross Detachment lived in a flat above a shop, she was awoken at 12.30 a.m. and she set about turning the flat into a rescue centre. *'Jimmy the Milk'* was able (from his milk orders) to give police details of people he knew were resident in Jaywick on that fateful weekend, Jimmy also saved a dog called *'Sally'*. I recommend you read the full account of the drama in the aforementioned Mary Lyons book. As for me, well I couldn't resist a look at *'Jaywick 2000'* and *'Spainy'* came along too.

AKA BRADSKYWALKER.

FRED IN LUTON REMEMBERS

No sooner had I mentioned Jaywick on the radio than Fred in Luton telephoned with a story, I asked him to write it for me:

"It was May 1939 and I was one of seven eighteen year old lads who hired a chalet on the front at Jaywick, it was called 'Owls Hoot'. Being all males and liking a drink it was pretty obvious that the Elsan would not cope with a whole week of seven fellow's 'natural disposals' therefore on a dark evening in the middle of the week two of the strongest members of our number did the only thing we could think of - we crossed the beach to effect an Elsan Evacuation! THE OWLS MUST HAVE A GOOD HOOT".

Fred in Luton, 1939 (before he learned French!)

You simply must visit Jaywick, I can't explain why, but you should. While you are in this corner of Essex make sure you take in Colchester. It's Britain's oldest recorded town and it has a castle as well as some Roman remains and there was a settlement in the area before the Romans arrived. The Iceni tribe led by Boudica, some people spell her name Boadicea but it makes little difference because she is long gone and won't argue. The Romans had been particularly tough on the Iceni and had killed Boudica's husband; she took control of the situation and, it is said, entered Colchester in her chariot with swords attached to the wheels, women drivers I ask you! She must have been pretty annoyed because she burned Colchester to the ground. The town was besieged for eleven weeks during the English Civil War and even suffered an earthquake in 1884.

Colchester is only some sixty miles from London. Telephone the Tourist Information Office on 01206 282920

During the 'Cold War' the government constructed regional government sites in case of nuclear attack and there are a couple of examples in the area. At Mistley near Manningtree you can enter one such construction, they have a couple of small cinemas where you can get the feel of what it must have been like in the 50's and 60's, sound effects add to the illusion. For more details telephone: 01206 395690

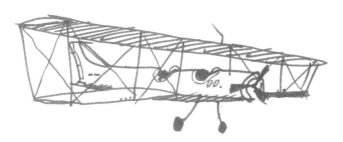

East Essex Aviation Society and Museum

Here you can see artefacts on show from the crash sites of wartime aircraft, there's the fuselage section of a Mustang fighter as well other civil and military historical items from both World Wars. 01255 428028 is the telephone number for further information.

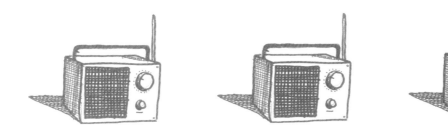

The National Vintage Wireless and Television Museum is in Harwich. It traces the history of broadcasting from Marconi and Baird to the present day. Telephone: 01206 322606

CONSTABLE THE LANDSCAPE ARTIST AND FLATFORD MILL

Artist John Constable is, of course well known for his paintings of the area. Probably his most famous work, 'The Hay Wain'. The mill you will see if you visit is not the original, but a Victorian replacement, Willy Lot's Cottage featured in the painting is still there though. Constable went to school in the village of Dedham just a short distance from East Bergholt.

Daughter Susie and wife Alice Spain at Flatford Mill

DEDHAM

The fine half timbered houses in Dedham High Street are a reminder of the prosperity that came to this village through the cloth industry. By a royal command in the 14th century the industry was created and craftsmen were brought in from Flanders to establish the fulling mills. The mills were used to cleanse the cloth and thicken it by beating and treading. The church of St Mary the Virgin stands on the site of a Saxon or Norman church. In 1492, when St Mary the Virgin was built, Dedham was at the very height of prosperity and the people of the town resolved to make it one of the finest churches in Essex, and of course it is also associated with John Constable (1776-1837) known throughout the world for his wonderful landscape painting. Nine miles northeast of Colchester you will find East Bergholt where the great man was born. His dad was a miller and he owned Flatford Mill where, in 1821 John Constable set up his easel to paint some of the beauty spots of East Anglia, including his local church. The tower is 131 feet high and the church is 144 feet in length and was much admired by John Constable. In the church are several heraldic shields, one is of the Royal Grammar School where Constable spent part of his childhood, also included are the arms of Dedham, Massachusetts; many people from Dedham emigrated with the Pilgrim fathers in 1620.

Views of Dedham Village, Essex, 2000

EAST HERTS FLYING SCHOOL

Whether you want to learn to fly for fun or a future career in Commercial Aviation

..here is the right place for you.

'Spainy' Takes to the Air!

The mere thought of David Spain in any aircraft smaller than a jumbo jet is somewhat sobering but it did happen and I was there to witness the event. I have to come clean with you at this point, 'Spainy' got me off the hook on this particular occasion. The plan was to make some recordings at historic Panshangar Airfield near the county town of Hertford, we would also take some photographs for use in the book, what a good idea! The airfield is still in use and was once a training field for the Royal Airforce back in the days when airman flew by the seat of their pants. It was however, the area of the seat of my pants that told me that I should not be the one to climb into something our instructor assured me was a plane. So I walked around the field with Geoff Overham as he told me what he knows of the history of Panshangar - as we walked my mind was racing faster than a Cessna's propeller, how could I get out of taking to the air? Would it ruin my image forever if I declined? If I didn't go would David Spain? Should I try to conquer my fear of heights? But first some of the history of Panshangar and its airfield.

By the time war broke out in 1939, the grass strip at Panshangar was already being used in a *'reserve capacity'* and the London Flying Club's operations were suspended until the cessation of hostilities. With De Havilland's at Hatfield building aircraft furiously for the war effort, Panshangar found its niche - it became a decoy airfield. Dummy hangars were created by Elstree Film Studios and camouflaged, the field was littered with cardboard vehicles and wooden aircraft which, it was hoped, would confuse the Luftwaffe. Panshangar also became a training base for the Royal Airforce as it became fully operational by 1942 complete with Tiger Moth aircraft. For me the great thing about Panshangar in the year 2000 is the Flying Club's office and reception. When 'Spainy' and I visited, the war time building was full of *'flying types'* glancing apprehensively at the weather and muttering about *'cloud cover'*. A wonderful log burning stove was belting out heat and one could just imagine pilots sitting outside in old armchairs and waiting for the word to *'scramble'*, however.... My enthusiasm did not extend to clambering into an aircraft! Oh dear no! Discretion became the better part of valour and I grudgingly (at least that's how I tried to make it look) gave up my seat in a Cessna to 'Spainy'. I remained on *'terra firma'* and took some photos as Geoff and David disappeared into the grey and overcast skies. As they drifted from view I wandered back to the 'Mess' for a cup of cocoa. Some twenty minutes later I heard the drone of an aircraft and hurried outside to take more pictures, a slightly green David fell rather unceremoniously from the aircraft (after it had landed of course) clutching his camera and muttering something about *"What a wonderful experience"*. Now I have been honest with you haven't I? As far as you are concerned, I could have told you that it was I who made the epic flight, but I didn't, so I will be equally honest (and this will ruin my street cred) and tell you that my first words to 'Spainy' were, *"I hadn't realised how attached I have become to you David, I was really concerned"*. My friend's response to this outbreak of affection was *"I bet you won't say that with your tape recorder switched on"* some people have no faith! All I can say is that he was lucky not to have been charged excess baggage!

Panshangar, used as a military airfield during the Second World War

Members and Staff of the Panshangar Airfield, 1999

East Herts Flying School is a flight training organisation approved by AOPA and the CAA. They offer professional instruction to all levels of ability on a modern fleet of Cessna and Piper Aircraft. Ground school is held in small groups in the friendly clubhouse, or alternatively, on a one to one basis to suit you.

Telephone: 01707 391791.

Spainy taxis off, while Pilgrim shivers

Digswell Viaduct, 1999

Aerial shots of the Hatfield, Stevenage and Hertford area

DIGSWELL

Close to the village of Welwyn you will find the Digswell Viaduct, it carries the main railway line from London to Edinburgh and spans the Mimram valley. Charles Blondin, the man who crossed Niagara Falls on a tightrope in 1859 practised here. In 1860 the silly Frenchman repeated his feat by crossing the falls with a wheelbarrow and a sack! Blondin was born in Hesdin, France on February 28th 1824. At the age of five he was sent to the Ecole de Gymnase at Lyon (quite why you would send you five year old son to such a school I cannot explain) anyway after just six months tiny tot Blondin, or to be more accurate Jean-Francois Gravelet (for that was his real name) made his first public appearance. During his lifetime Blondin, also known as 'The Little Wonder' crossed the falls at Niagara several times. He once sat down and cooked an omelette half way! But of course he was French! In 1861 Blondin turned somersaults on stilts on a rope stretched across the main transept of the Crystal Palace. Blondin died at Little Ealing near London in 1897.

Should you chance to cross the viaduct, and I suggest you do so by train and not 'a la Blondin', you will no doubt notice Digswell Lake and an area of ornamental gardens covering around seventeen acres. It is maintained by members of the Digswell Lake Society. The Church of St. John at Digswell, is eight hundred years old and some of the remains of the 12th century walls can still be seen, there are also some brasses of some interest.

BENGEO

I played a few games of cricket in Bengeo when I was working at nearby Chapmore End. I also had a few pints with actor Brian Wilde in the 'local', nice chap Brian, best remembered as the 'soft' prison warder in 'Porridge' and as 'Foggy' in 'Last of the Summer Wine'. Despite the close proximity of Hertford, Bengeo retains a lot of its distinct village character. Bengeo Hall is timber framed and some parts of the building date back some five hundred years. Archers practised on the meads below the Warren during the 16th century and I struggled up the hill from Hertford in a 1930 Morris convertible in the 20th! (don't ask). Thomas Dimsdale who experimented with inoculations lived in the village, he used what is now known as the 'Pest House' for his tests. Thomas became Baron Dimsdale as a result of inoculating the Empress of Russia and her family, now that is an interesting fact isn't it? And so just to end this little piece on Bengeo here is a poem written by one Corporal Lobb of the Bengeo Home Guard:

'We possess countless privates called Vigus
And it is not that they don't li'gus
They are absent from drill
And we know that they will
Milk their cows first, then fight like old tigers'

HERTFORD

Julius Caesar first visited Britain in 55 BC and there was already a settlement on the banks of the Lea in what is now Hertfordshire. The Angles and the Saxons invaded from Germany in the fifth century and Heortoford as it was known attracted the East Saxons. Heortoford means *'the place where the hart or male red deer forded the river'*

and, as we all know the Hart remains on the crest of the county badge to this day. The first general synod of the Church of England was held in Hertford in the year 673, the synod was the precursor of Parliament. Edward the Elder, son of Alfred the Great rebuilt Hertford in 914 after his dad had driven out the Danes. Thomas Smith is the man responsible for the Tower in the town, it is in fact a folly built in the late 19th century. Thomas was an architect and also designed the County Hospital and Christ Church. He married Elizabeth Bellchambers whose family had a shop in Hertford, and eventually Thomas Smith became Mayor in 1868. There is still plenty to see and enjoy on Hertford, they have re-designed the town centre and somewhat changed the feel of it. When we lived nearby in the seventies, Hertford was a very rustic county town, populated by people wearing corduroy trousers, caps and heavy knit sweaters (and that was just the women!). I took a walk around the town with some members of the local history society a couple of years ago and one chap simply couldn't wait to relate the grisly happenings of yesteryear. I recommend you try to arrange such a walk yourself, it really is an eye-opener.

Main Square in Hertford

Eating out 'continental style', Hertford

Hertford Castle

FUNNY YOU SHOULD MENTION BIGGLES!

It has been said many times before and I have little doubt it will be said again, I have the sort of mind that stores away information that will never be used, except that sometime it might be. The day after David Spain had emulated Lindbergh, Amy Johnson and the Wright Brothers all rolled into one (and I use the word '*rolled*' advisedly), I was gazing idly at my computer screen trying to think what to write next. How could I link my friend's flying exploits with the next story? **BIGGLES! THAT'S HOW**. You see I remembered that the creator of some of the most exciting stories I ever read as a child was born in the county town of Hertford (well Bengeo just outside Hertford to be more precise), not a couple of miles from Panshangar. Before you could say '*Out and About*' I was on the telephone to Hertford library, they told me that the expert on Captain W. E. Johns (for those who spent a deprived childhood, 'twas he who created Biggles, Algy and Worralls) was a lady named Jennifer Schofield. Before you could say '*David Spain is overweight*' I was speaking to Jennifer on the telephone, "*Yes*" she would speak on my radio programme and "*Yes*" she would send me a copy of her book on the worthy captain, thank you Jennifer.

It has been claimed that many World War II Spitfire pilots claimed to have learned their aerial manoeuvres from the '*Biggles*' books! At first this statement appears to be difficult to believe but when you learn something of the life of Captain W.E. Johns it becomes more plausible. William Earl Johns was born in 1893 at Bengeo, Hertfordshire, his father was a tailor and his mother the daughter of a master butcher. I doubt that Richard and Elizabeth dreamt that their son would grow up to become the author of nearly a hundred '*Biggles*' books. It seems equally unlikely that they would have expected that young William would find the time to write a gardening column, produce science fiction and adult thrillers and become a rather useful artist as well. W.E. Johns managed to cram rather a lot into his seventy five years on this earth (and above it come to that). During the First World War he was an aviator of considerable skill and survived several dogfights and crashes, he was also a prisoner of war.

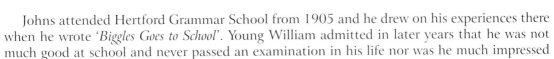

Johns attended Hertford Grammar School from 1905 and he drew on his experiences there when he wrote '*Biggles Goes to School*'. Young William admitted in later years that he was not much good at school and never passed an examination in his life nor was he much impressed

by matters of a mechanical nature, but he could shoot straight, hitting the bulleseye nine times out of ten at a distance of a thousand yards. On leaving school our young hero was indentured to a municipal surveyor, he also made some extra cash by playing the piano in the local cinema, no signs yet then, of the life to come. In 1912, Johns left home to become a sanitary inspector in the Norfolk town of Swaffham, he became bored with life and joined the Territorial Army. World events took a hand in William's life when war was declared in August 1914. Johns never talked much about the three years he spent in the trenches and who can blame him? He applied for a transfer to the Royal Flying Corps on the basis of what he experienced and reaching the conclusion that there was '*no point in dying standing up in squalor if one could do so sitting down in clean air*'.

His first solo flight proved to be a disaster, Johns own record reveals that it lasted some five seconds and reached a height of thirty feet before crashing back to terra firma!

But, as thousands of boys (young and old) will still testify to this day, the characters W.E. Johns created would be a source of pleasure and inspiration throughout their childhood. '*Biggles*', '*Worralls*', '*Gimlett*', '*Steeley*' and others appeared on the radio and TV and the cinema screen. David Spain has decided to subscribe to 'Biggles Flies Again', a magazine edited by Jennifer Schofield, I recommend you join '*Spainy*', you can contact Jennifer on: 01243 671209

THE YEAR 1606 AND ALL THAT!

In 1606 the people living in and around Stanstead Abbots saw fit to complain about the smell, they were, it is said *'constrained to stop their noses as they go bye, the stinke is so great'* and the reason? Woad. I don't know a great deal about Woad (I quite like *'Middle of the Woad'* music though). I know that our forefathers saw fit to daub themselves in it from time to time and that it is a member of the mustard family (as indeed are the Colemans!) and that it grows in America. It is also said that as Woad was processed to make dye, the smell became more *'attractive'* which is probably more than can be said for those who chose to wear the stuff! It is also quite possible that some of my forefathers worked with Woad because my great, great, great grandfather and grandmother, Joseph and Mary (and before you ask, no, none of my ancestors were born in a stable) are buried at Stanstead Abbots Church. It is claimed that there has been a church on the site since before Domesday, it's a flint and rubble construction and the tower was built by William Stowell, the master mason of Westminster Abbey. Stanstead Abbots Church is situated high on a hill just outside the town.

Joseph and Mary parented seven girls and five boys. My great, great grandfather (another Joseph, not very original the Pilgrims') was a journeyman miller in the village while Seth his older brother followed his father's profession of shoemaker. The two boys moved to Brentford in 1840, it is more than likely that they hitched a lift on the weekly barley delivery barge down the River Lea and onto Brentford. Seth returned home to die in the Ware Union Workhouse in June 1875. Joseph remained in Brentford to further the family line, times would have been hard but Joseph persevered (fortunately for me) and I am but one testimony to his strength and endurance, indeed five other siblings peer over my shoulder as I write!

Naturally David Spain is somewhat amused at the thought of my family covering their bodies in Woad (working class Woad of course) and charging about the Hertfordshire countryside. You should not allow this thought to stop you from visiting Stanstead Abbots and the church.

Stanstead Abbots Church

LETCHWORTH - SOME PERSONAL MEMORIES

Chris Hargreaves lives in Letchworth, Hertfordshire and wrote to tell me about his childhood memories. It's his story so I decided to let him tell it.

"In 1949 my step father decided to kick us out, it was just after my brother Phil was born, we - that is myself aged eight, Robin aged ten, Daphne aged five and brother Phil were sent to the Grange, a children's home opposite the 'Bowling Green' in Stevenage, my mum went to what, I think was a home for single parents, she took baby Phil with her. At the Grange we were given a bath (all in the same bath) and rubbed vigorously with coal tar soap and a huge scrubbing brush. In bed that night my brothers and sisters cried themselves to sleep as did I, Phil being the eldest tried to maintain a 'stiff upper lip'.

My mum visited us about once a month and those visits were the happiest part of the next fifteen months of our young lives. On Saturday mornings we were given rags to wrap around our feet so that we could polish the floor, I really enjoyed the polishing because it was fun to slide around the floor. I used to walk to Letchworth to see my eldest brother who was living with an aunt, I was eight years old at the time but the walk was never questioned. On one occasion I walked with two friends to see their mum in Ware, when we arrived back at the Grange we were given six strokes of the cane. We went to school from the Grange and although I can't recall the name of the school, I did visit it some forty years later to carry out some work and one (now very old) teacher recognised me. I remember very vividly one girl who was about twelve years old, she ruled us kids with a rod of iron. A couple of kids whose names I can't remember used to have visits from their mother, she would bring her two babies with her and breast feed them both at the same time!

In general I think that the staff did what they could for us but several of us ran wild. Some kids used to break into the Vincent factory and steal parts which they then sold to the motor cycle shop over the road, the proceeds would get us into the 'Publix' cinema and leave something over to purchase milk lollies and other goodies from 'Mollies'. After something like fifteen months we received news that we were to move to Heath Lodge, Royston to be re-united with mum and our brother Paul. Six of us all moved into one room, there were about thirty people in all living at Heath Lodge and we shared one toilet and one bath between us, wire netting was spread from the balcony, presumably to stop people throwing themselves off in despair! Since we were fairly conspicuous we all stuck together when we went to school, we were known as 'The workhouse boys'.

In 1951 we were given a council house in Letchworth and brother Eddie returned to the fold, much to the delight of our aunt and uncle I suspect! The local MP Nigel Fisher who had helped us get the house visited us and we also received food parcels from the American Forces at Bassingbourn Barracks. I look back on those days with some affection and my mum (now aged 86) still likes to sit with me and remember".

ROY'S WARTIME MEMORIES

When Roy Williams retired he decided to record his childhood memories of World War Two, not only did he make a written record but he employed his talent as an artist.

Summer 1940 - Ten Year Old Roy's Story

"One day I was eating my lunch when I heard an aircraft approaching fairly low from the direction of Hitchin, I ran outside to see what type of plane it was (from the engine noise I suspected that it would be German). During that Summer the weather was glorious but on this particular day there was a low cloud base. I saw a German Dornier break through the murk and what's more it seemed to be heading directly at me! I stared in horror as the pale blue plane with huge black crosses on the side approached. I realised that I could see him, then some crew member, possibly behind a machine gun, could see me, so I dashed back indoors. I couldn't resist a peep from the safety of our back door and watched as the plane disappeared behind some more low cloud. Shortly after this incident, I heard that the Vauxhall works in Luton had been bombed by Heinkel 111's so it is possible that 'my' Dornier was on a local reconnaissance of the target prior to the bombing raid. I understand that the main office block at Vauxhall was hit and that the bombs destroyed parts of the central staircase, making evacuation of casualties difficult".

At the side of the road running past the works stands a monument bearing panels with the names of those who were killed on that August day in 1940.

A SPITFIRE NAMED LETCHWORTH

During the hot summer of 1940, aircraft losses to both the RAF and the Luftwaffe were heavy and the aircraft industries of both countries worked round the clock to make up those losses. In the late summer of 1940 the loss of a Messerschmitt 109E German fighter helped the RAF to gain a Spitfire. Roy Williams takes up the story.

"The government had set up a 'Spitfire Fund' where ordinary people could contribute money raised through social events to 'buy' a Spitfire. A forced down Messerschmitt was brought to the Arena, which was a grassed area between the Co-Op store in Eastcheap and the council offices. Wooden hoardings were set up around the German plane so that only those paying sixpence at the entrance could see the plane. I collected my pennies and hurried to the enclosure, paid my entry fee and was confronted by the sinister black crosses and swastika fin emblem at close quarters. I was able to look at the compact cockpit and would have just loved to get my young hands on those controls! After poking my nose into every available nook and cranny I went home satisfied that the enemy aircraft had been 'downed' by a Spitfire. The town of Letchworth raised £5,000 by late 1940 and a Spitfire was allocated to carry the town's name into battle. A contemporary photograph published in a local newspaper in October 1941 is careful to hide the front of the wings but the blister on the top surface to house a larger cannon can be seen, it would not have given away the fact that this Spitfire was Mk VB version. 'Letchworth' survived the war and was then sold to Portugal. When I retired I thoroughly researched 'Spitfire Letchworth' and have since made an oil painting of the subject".

SOMETIMES IT JUST HAPPENS

The very nature of the radio version of *'Out and About'* means that you never really know what a caller is going to tell you and so it was one afternoon (I can't remember why) I asked if anyone had witnessed aerial *'dogfights'* during the war years.

The very next telephone call I took led me to believe that we were going to hear a story about ordinary people arresting a German spy. It seems that one day an aerial fight took place over Dagenham (what ever happened to the girl pipers?) - Gordon from Stevenage told how the people on the ground saw a parachute open during the course of a *'dogfight'*, believing that a Nazi plane had been hit they rushed to their garden sheds to arm themselves with spades and forks. The unfortunate pilot landed in the middle of a road and the locals quickly spotted that he was dressed in civilian clothes. The suspect was surrounded by an angry crowd, he shouted at them as he lay on the ground but they couldn't understand what he was saying, they pressed closer waving garden implements at him. It was a bus driver who saved the day, jumping from his cab the driver threw himself across the prone body of the flier, *'I understand what he is saying, he is not a German spy!'* shouted the driver. It turned out that the pilot was in fact a young Scotsman and so was the bus driver! It seems that the pilot had been off duty when he was asked to take a plane to another base and had not had time to get into his uniform. Such stories from the war years have enlightened many an afternoon on *'Out and About'*.

Posh Gordon with his Dad

I have called Gordon from Stevenage 'Posh' ever since he purchased a mobile telephone! Gordon and I have been talking on the radio since the days when I presented the early morning programme for Three Counties Radio. We met face to face when Gordon came to the Millenium Festival at Shuttleworth near Bedford, he brought along his dog '*Jess*' as well because '*Jess*' is very much a part of Gordon's life. I asked Gordon to write a short history of his dad's life after hearing some of the stories.

'*My Dad*' born Cliffe- at- Hooe, Kent, November 1900.

1912 During his school holidays my father sailed as third hand on his uncle's Thames Sailing Barge carrying a cargo of cement from the Isle of Grain across to Ostend, returning with a cargo of wheat.

1914 On the day he left school his headmaster gave dad '*fourteen of the best*' seven on each hand, telling him that they were for the misdemeanours that he had not been caught for!   World War I started and dad lied about his age and joined up, when grandmother found out she brought him home. He got a job as a fireman on a Foden Steam Wagon delivering cement from Dagenham to places like Letchworth which was a one day round trip - at twelve miles per hour Birmingham took two days! The driver was taken ill on a run to Birmingham and dad drove the wagon home! As a reward the manager gave dad the money to purchase his licence.

In **1918** dad joined the army again, he was in the First Battalion Coldstream Guards and became part of the escort for the Crown Prince, he was rewarded with a walking cane bearing the Royal Coat of Arms, unfortunately this memento was sold to provide money for food for my mother and sister during the General Strike.

Baby 'Posh' Gordon and Dad 1931

1920 Awarded the Royal Humane Society Certificate for saving a man from drowning in the Thames at Greenwich. When he arrived home after the incident he didn't tell anyone and so received a smack around the ear from his mum for ruining his best suit (my paternal grandmother must have packed quite a punch, she stood six feet three and weighed eighteen stone!).

1925 Married my mother and became an L.C.C. Tram Driver after the 1926 General Strike. One day the tram brakes failed on a steep hill and there was a crash. The management told dad that if wanted to keep his job he should take the blame; the police told him that if accepted liability they would arrest him. The matter was settled when the Inquiry Board went to inspect the tram and found it ablaze and all the evidence destroyed!

1930 Dad bluffed his way into a job as a crane driver at the Ford Motor Company. In those days the company could send you a telegram when you were on holiday ordering you to return to work. Employees who lived across the river were ferried across by rowing boat and in foggy weather a man stood in the bow with a lantern and megaphone.

1939 At the outbreak of World War Two, dad was classed as working in a reserved occupation so he enlisted in the Auxiliary Fire Service until the Local Defence Volunteers were formed. When the Home Guard replaced the LDV, dad because of his Guard's experience was made a sergeant, his platoon comprised of dockers and Billingsgate fish porters. One night dad was standing on the jetty during an air attack, a bomb exploded nearby and he was blown off his feet stunning him. When he recovered his senses he found himself in water swimming like mad but unable to move. *"My god"* he thought *"I'm in the river and I'm paralysed"*, he bellowed for help and a voice replied *"Get up you silly sod, you're lying in a puddle under the Fire Engine"*.

1942 Dad volunteered for the Royal Navy where he attained the rank of Petty Officer Coxswain of a Landing Barge Oiler.

June 6th 1944 His flotilla was leaving harbour when a German bomber jettisoned its bombs, the stick fell astern of his craft which just happened to be carrying 10,000 gallons of aviation spirit. Dad explained *"As the bombs came down we went over the side"*. They received seven days survivors leave, we never heard this story until after the war. At the time dad told us that they didn't have a job for him so they sent him home for a week!
When he did return to the fray he worked at supplying hospital ships, he was unable to locate his flotilla and toured up and down the coast from Cherbourg to Antwerp and Ostend searching for them. He was told by another cox'n that they had been destroyed on D. Day. He was demobbed in 1945 and returned to his job as a crane driver until he retired in 1967. My mum suffered a stroke and was hospitalised in 1972, dad attended to her daily needs until he could not stand the decline in hospital services, so he discharged mum and cared for her until she died in 1977. In 1983 dad suffered a stroke but recovered, much to the surprise of his doctors, he moved into sheltered accommodation in Stevenage and lived there until he passed away in 1988. With the help of the Metropolitan Police (Thames Division) my wife and I scattered his ashes on the River Thames by the Royal Naval College at Greenwich where he earned his Royal Humane Society Certificate.

I thank Gordon for telling us his dad's story; for me it serves to demonstrate the debt of gratitude we all owe the people of that generation.

NICK

We have seen some examples of Roy William's artistic talent, so it is time to take a break and meet a young artist who is making his way in the world. I have known Nick Milstead since he went to school with my daughter Johanna. You will have seen his cartoons in our first *'Out and About'* book as well as this one. Cartoons are a very small example of young Mr. Milstead's talent.

Nick's work can be seen on **www.mustardmag.org** (free magazine similar to 'Private Eye') or to contact Nick Telephone: **020 84550988**
   email: **nicksart7@hotmail.com**

ENTOMBED IN A BEDOUIN TENT

My brother Bill had set up some recordings in Mortlake, because I had decided to take the *'Out and About'* programme beyond Beds, Herts and Bucks and *'bruv'* told me that Mortlake has an interesting history, indeed it has and what's more.....

I arrived in Mortlake on a somewhat dull and damp Monday morning and Bill explained that he had discovered a rather interesting last resting place in the local cemetery (I don't mean that it was to be Bill's last resting place, because he's not ready to go yet, I mean that it was already someone else's resting place). Bill had arranged an interview with a man who has worked at St Mary Magdalen Roman Catholic Church for some years and so it came to pass that I conducted an interview in a converted World War Two air raid shelter! Ted Mc Cormack invited us into his *'study'* where just about anything and everything is stored. Needless to say that there was no window, air raid shelters did not come equipped with the means to view the outside world. It was only about 10 a.m. but Ted offered us a *'wee dram'* of whisky, not wishing to appear rude we accepted (but sipped rather than *'slurped'*). I have to admit that I did find myself wondering exactly what we were doing in such a place rather than discovering the history of Mortlake but Bill had assured me that all would be revealed (I don't mean that Bill was going to reveal all, I mean that the story would become clear).

Interred in the cemetery of St Mary Magdalen are the remains of one Sir Richard Francis Burton, scholar, explorer and Orientalist. It was Burton who became the first European to discover Lake Tanganyika and Burton who explored hitherto forbidden Muslim cities. What a life this man had led, but I had to wait a little longer before I was to view his coffin (yes, you can see the coffin) because our Ted insisted my brother and I should join him in another dram before we braved the cold and somewhat overgrown churchyard. We didn't mind much because the story of Burton is intriguing.

Born in Torquay, Devon in 1821, Burton was of Irish / English parentage, his father retired early from the army and moved the family to mainland Europe to raise young Richard and his brother and sister. Richard proved to be an amazing scholar, he became fluent in French, Italian and the Bearnais and Neapolitan dialects (don't ask me what Bearnais and Neapolitan dialects are because I don't know, I thought they were ice creams!). A minor breach of discipline (I can't elaborate because I haven't got the details, so you can wonder along with me), young Richard went to India as an officer in the Regiment of Bombay Native Infantry, he mastered Arabic and Hindi and became proficient in Marathi, Sindhi, Punjabi, Pashto and Multani (I know, I know just imagine how useful he would be in your local takeaway!). With dialects included, Burton learned over forty languages. Burton was asked by the commander of the English forces in Sindhi to disguise himself and investigate the homosexual brothels of Karachi - I can't say just why his commander required such details, sufficient to state that Burton's somewhat explicit report seems to have brought about the end of his army career! He returned to England ill and unhappy.

Richard, now aged 29, moved to France where he lived with his mother and sister, he wrote four books on India and put together plans to visit Mecca. I hope that like me you are amazed at the life of this man Burton because there is so much more to come. In 1853 he went to Cairo, Suez and Medina, he also visited the sacred city of Mecca and made drawings of the mosque and the shrine there. In 1855 Burton put together an expedition to discover the source of the White Nile. The White Nile plans were destined to bring Burton great disappointment. Between 1857 and 1858 (after he had fought as a volunteer in the Crimean

War) he led an expedition with John Hanning Speke (more of Speke later). The explorers took each and every privation the continent of Africa could throw at them. When they eventually made it to the shores of Lake Tanganyika, Burton was so ill from Malaria that he could not walk and Speke was virtually blind. The local natives told them that the Rusizi River flowed into the lake rather than out of it and, though Burton wanted to make a new expedition, Speke (who had recovered from his ailments more quickly than Burton) went on alone to discover Lake Victoria. Speke convinced himself and others that this was the source of the Nile, the two adventurers quarrelled and Speke returned to England before his erstwhile friend. Burton became something of an outcast among those who saw themselves as supporters of explorers and adventurers while Speke was idolised. In 1860 our hero went to America where he visited the Mormon stronghold of Salt Lake City, he subsequently wrote '*The City of the Saint*' and proved that he could write on American subjects equally as well as he could on others. In 1861, after his return from America, Burton married (secretly) Isabel Arundell the daughter of a well to do (aristocratic) family. The feud between Burton and Speke continued and became a public topic of conversation. Burton became Consul in Trieste, a job he really didn't aspire to. Between 1872 and his death he continued to write books on archaeology, Iceland (yes Iceland, now, I ask you, whoever wrote a book on Iceland?) the gold mines of Midian and some of his best poetry.

Burton's tomb (and that of his wife who died in 1896) is designed in the manner of a Bedouin tent, there are some iron steps at the rear of the tomb to enable visitors to take a look inside. It is said that seances have been held inside the tomb but I found no proof of this, I am told that following her husband's death, Isabel used to sit inside the tomb. To this day an annual Mass is said for Sir Richard Burton on 22nd January - the date of his marriage to Isabel.

The tomb of Sir Richard Burton, (scholar and explorer) at Mortlake

BAKED BEANS WITH BENNY

Benny Green was a hero of mine but I approached my interview with him with some trepidation. I am still not sure why I was concerned, after all I had been invited to Benny's home in Kings Langley and he knew what we were going to talk about, nevertheless I knocked on the front door of my hero's home somewhat nervously. I needn't have worried, Benny invited me to join him in his study and offered to share his lunch time snack of beans on toast! I knew just how I was going to break the ice, we shared a passion for cricket and for a pleasant half hour we discussed great moments from our youth and choosing our all time 'great' England team. Benny Green was born on December 9th, 1927 in Leeds (not in London as most people would assume), Benny's mum had moved to her parents home to have her baby. The family lived in Greenwell Street, London in a somewhat run down area predominately inhabited by Jewish and Italian families. The family soon moved to Cleveland Street where the young Mr Green spent his formative years in a basement flat. Benny probably inherited his love for music from his father Dave who played jazz with an orchestra in Leeds.

When you interview a person on tape it is necessary to sit quite close to them and as I chatted with Benny Green I was struck by the lack of colour in his face, I couldn't have known that my hero was not long for this world. I, like many of my age remember Benny as a great writer on many subjects (including cricket) as well as a superb musician but, for me it will always be the wonderful radio moments he created. I recall many happy hours sitting alone with my radio listening to Benny describe music in the most magical manner, he was quite clearly totally besotted with his subject and communicated this fact to his listeners. Benny Green and his family lived at Langley House, Kings Langley for many years and he became very much part of daily life in the village. I know that he could be a bit 'grouchy' at times, particularly when he felt his privacy was being invaded but I also know that he took a great interest in the people around him. I was told by an elderly ex soldier that Benny would invite him to spend a day at Christmas at Langley House.

Just as I was about to leave Benny's home I asked him what he thought of the recently released best selling album of George Gershwin numbers, I knew that Gershwin was a favourite of his and was hoping to impress the great man with my musical knowledge. Benny stroked his chin and asked me to tell him more, I informed him that Larry Adler had put together the album with such luminaries as Elton John, Sting and Oleta Adams. Benny stroked his chin again "*Never heard of it boy*" he said. I promised to play a couple of tracks on my Sunday afternoon show just for him. The following week I received a note at the studios "*Thanks John*" it said and was signed Benny.

AKA · BRAD SKYWALKER

A Trip to Norway

Listener James Allan called in one afternoon to relate a fascinating tale about his visit to Norway. No simple sea cruise eating open sandwiches or taking the sea air on deck for our James! When David Spain and I visited James at his Kings Langley home we were presented with documentary evidence of his story from 1940.

When James Allan joined the Royal Airforce he knew that it wouldn't be to fly aircraft because of his poor eyesight but he was given a revolver and a nice holster! James is understandably a little vague on some points but a visit to the RAF Museum at Hendon and James's own records reveal what happened after his brief training period with the Royal Air Force, he found himself on a boat! Along with the rest of the crew and some marines and airforce types, James was informed that their ship was heading for Norway. Since Hitler had already invaded that country Mr Allan (and no doubt most of his colleagues) felt that their journey was, to say the least, likely to be somewhat unhealthy. Suffice to say that after landing close to Lake Lesjaskog in the land of the Norsemen the lads set up camp and carted ashore a great deal of aircraft fuel. Still in the dark as to the purpose of their mission, they were joined by a number of Gloster Gladiator aircraft. Sporting his fine revolver James was informed that they were *"going to have a go at Jerry"*. Now you will remember that James was not a flyer so why was he on a lake in Norway? Well to this day he can't be really sure, the officer who had been with him during training did go to Norway as well but James saw nothing more of him after their arrival. In *'civvy street'* the young master Allan had worked in a great house as a *'general factotum'* and was under the impression that he was recruited to act in a similar fashion for this officer chappie, hence the revolver. Things started to get a little hot in Norway, one day an aircraft was spotted and a couple of Marines chose to ignore James when he informed them that it was British, the plane was shot down with a Bofors Gun, thankfully the pilot bailed out. The Luftwaffe decided to pay our boys a visit as well and some of the Gloster Gladiators were attacked as they stood on the frozen lake, they sank without trace. Soon afterwards James and his comrades undertook a long trek through the Norwegian countryside (just the sort of walk you wouldn't fancy with the German army breathing down your neck) and arrived at a fjord, here they were taken out to sea in a small boat and then ordered to clamber aboard a British Navy ship. James found himself in the Scapa Flow but they didn't disembark, their ship made its way to the Clyde via *"half of the Atlantic"* according to James.

Douglas Fairbanks Jnr. visits James in hospital

ROYAL AIR FORCE MUSEUM - HENDON

I paid a visit to Hendon to take a look at one of the Gloster Gladiators that James Allan mentioned in his story of Norway. It's hard to believe that such an aircraft was once a weapon of war, the Gladiator on show was raised from the Norwegian lake after the war. There is so much to see at Hendon that a single visit is simply not enough.

Harrier Jump Jet on display at Hendon Museum

Gloucester Gladiator by lake in Norway, 1940

Gloucester Gladiator salvaged from lake

WISH YOU WERE HERE, MAYBE YOU ARE?

I Know An Old Gentleman With Ash Blonde Hair

At least he tells me that his hair is Ash blonde, I insist that it's grey ! His name is Ernie Almond. I met 'Ern' when I first joined the radio station and despite changing my telephone number at least three times, my address twice and my identity once he has managed to keep tabs on me. He has many strengths, at least that is what he never tires of telling me and recently he has mastered the art of e mailing, this means that I am bombarded with whole lists of jokes every night of the week. Ernie Almond appeared in the first 'Out and About' book when I informed readers that I liked him, this was a big mistake because he sent me his account of how we met.

"I started knocking at the door of the BBC building on the ring road in Luton almost before the cement was dry! Having been a professional entertainer since 1970, I just couldn't understand how the management of local radio imagined that they would last five minutes without my enormous talent. After pestering them for some time the BBC eventually let me in - only to send me straight out again (as often as possible) with a tape recorder, usually to record one of the local amateur dramatic society's spectacular renditions of the 'Pirates of Penzance'. This was usually performed to the accompaniment of the village undertaker on the piano and Mrs Critchley (taking an evening off from the petrol pumps) on the drums. After just a few fleeting years the 'beeb' let me progress to making comedy (at least I thought they were) trails and jingles for other programmes. I also provided the voice for a teddy bear! In those days Saturday nights would find me in the studios playing various characters for a programme called "Smeet Petite and the Karachi Kid" (yes, even my mind boggles at the thought of it). But I really thought that I had arrived - how mistaken can you be? Why I hadn't even met John Pilgrim yet!

One dark night, close to the hour of midnight I was busy recording the blessed teddy bear being kidnapped by pirates and having to play all the parts myself including the "Motley Crew" when in walks this kindly old gent. I greeted him warmly and directed him to the car park commenting that he probably wouldn't need to be on duty before daylight. "No! No!" says he "I'm here to broadcast". Well you could have knocked me over with an old EP! He didn't look anything like a broadcaster, he had absolutely no sign of recording tape trailing from his back pocket, or even a chinagraph pencil behind his ear! How he ever thought he could make the grade without these two essential items I still haven't fathomed to this day! We had a chat over a cuppa and he asked me a few "Where do they keep this or that" questions - which of course I refused to answer for fear of upsetting the management, I was concerned that it might leak out that BBC staff are expected to supply their own pencils! He told me that he was at the studios to record a series of quiz programmes leading up to one called "The Car Boot Quiz". I tried to warn him (as did many other members of staff) that a trivia quiz with music, giving away prizes purchased from a car boot sale would never work. Had it not been for the fact that the show became one of the most popular programmes we have ever broadcast on a Sunday, I think he would have believed me!

Anyway to make a short story much longer, that was the beginning of a very good friendship both on and off air. I spent three very happy years co-presenting "The Club on a Saturday Night" with John and helping out with many early "Out and About" programmes. I have a host of memories, like J.P. playing "The Stripper" music as I entered the studio, dancing with the regular listeners at an imaginary barbeque, recording in the village of Harlington at six degrees below with my hand frozen to the microphone, trying to broadcast live from the top of Ivinghoe Beacon while the wind was making more noise than we were! Yes a host of memories, all looked back on now with great affection".

Ernie (on left) interviews Steve McFadden (Phil Mitchell in 'Eastenders')

Ernie and JP held at Her Majesty's Pleasure and not theirs!

BUSHEY - A MUSEUM - A MAN NAMED WOOD - A MAN NAMED HERKOMER

I like Bushey because, despite everything the developers have tried, it is still a village and a great credit to the people who have worked so hard to preserve it. The museum is always worth a visit because they are always adding to it. My visits are supervised by Mr Bryen Wood who firmly believes that Bushey is the centre of the universe! The museum was opened in October 1993 and that same year was awarded first prize in the Gulbenkian Foundation Awards.

Bushey Museum, former Urban District Council Offices built in 1909

Presentation by Herr Franz Rössle, Mayor of twin-town Landsberg-am-Lech

Bushey High Street, cottages on left demolished in 1913, which is now the present Green

Born in Bavaria, Buried in Bushey

Sir Hubert von Herkomer was the son of a poor wood carver and piano teacher. His family emigrated first to America and then England. Hubert trained at South Kensington Art School and became a society and court painter of some note. He also painted documentary pictures of the poor and elderly. Herkomer founded an art school in a kind of reaction to his own somewhat limited education, the art school ran for over twenty years and was highly successful. A somewhat restless man, Herkomer became interested in theatre and film, he was involved in many new printing processes including *'Mezzotint'*. It seemed inevitable that this *'workaholic'* innovator would move into film making and indeed he did. Although it was a somewhat brief career it proved successful, prior to Herkomer's involvement in movie making the upper classes had seen the medium as a little vulgar. He constructed one of the very first *'Daylight'* studios in this country,(in Bushey) in fact it later became one of the oldest working studios in Europe. Herkomer contributed a great deal to the life of Bushey, not simply through his film making but in the buildings he created. On an estate in Bushey he built *'Lululaund'* a mock Bavarian castle, designed as a memorial to his beloved wife *'Lulu'*. Herkomer was married three times, his first wife gave him two children before she died in 1882. It is rumoured that *'Lulu'* had been his mistress and following the death of wife number one Herkomer married *'Lulu'*, after a year *'Lulu'* died and Herkomer was devastated, hence *'Lululaund'*. A third marriage followed (this time to Lulu's sister) and they had two children. When *'Spainy'* and I visited Bushey we were given a guided tour of the Museum and the village. Not much of *'Lululaund'* is left, just a chunk of the front of the house in fact. Herkomer was quite a man, materials for the house were brought from Germany and the interior was a rather dark gothic place. Houses were built on the estate as Herkomer didn't much care for the servants *'living in'* so, if he required a drink or some other service during the night, the servant would be called to the great house. A very busy and talented man was Hubert von Herkomer, it may be that he sponsored the first *'Grand Prix'* which probably became the *"Monte Carlo Rally"*. The great man is buried in Bushey churchyard, his grave is a fitting place to end your walk around the village.

Tony Hopkins, JP, Bryen at 'Lululaund'

The former 'Daylight' Studio, Bushey

THE IMPORTANCE OF MISS COE

I told you that Bryen Wood considers Bushey to be the centre of the universe didn't I? Well the man who made that statement also tells me that a certain Miss Coe is to blame!

"Miss Coe had been an infant at Rutts School in Bushey Heath, had later returned as a pupil teacher and then stayed on there for the rest of her working life. I went to The Rutts in 1940, when I was four and she read us stories about how people had lived in the past. I can remember little about The Rutts except those stories and they influenced my whole life.

In 1943 I went to Ashfield School, a somewhat old fashioned place but I managed to pass the examination for Watford Grammar School and I started there at the age of eight. I wanted to study history but was persuaded to read law at the LSE.

I wanted to be an Inspector of Ancient Monuments (If he had been Bryen could have inspected 'Spainy') but you had to know the right people, or I wanted to be a museum curator but you could not live on the salary. I did spells as a chef, a turner, a security guard, and ended up at Kodak. I enjoyed the intellectual challenge of the jobs at Kodak but felt I wasn't making my mark on the world.

Archaeology and history had to be a hobby, to be fitted in with the family and keeping our ancient house in Bushey High Street from falling down. My interest in history focused on Bushey and Watford, neither of which had a museum at the time, I collected old photographs and ephemera and information. There was some local interest but not on a large scale. In the 1970's a group of us were asked to put on local history exhibitions for charity and we were pleasantly surprised at the response. Bushey has a unique history for an otherwise obscure village, of some two hundred years of art teaching of various times. From the Monro Circle in the early 19th century through to the Herkomer School, the Lucy Kemp-Welch Schools, the Frobisher School and many other smaller schools. Many hundreds of artists have lived and worked in Bushey. Our group collected their pictures as best we could but in contrast to local ephemera, serious money was too often involved.

One day in 1983, as we dismantled yet another temporary exhibition, we asked ourselves what were we doing? The obvious had taken some time to perceive! We should have our own museum in Bushey! We formed a charitable Museum Trust and asked Hertsmere Council for help. What was so obvious to us was not as obvious to the council, but they did declare their support in principle (but no money). However they did give us some storage space at the Old Council Offices in Rudolph Road and that was a good start.

The next ten years were spent in wresting small sums of money and wringing concessions from a sceptical council. Meanwhile the accountants had taken over at Kodak and I organised myself early retirement in 1993. Later that year we opened Bushey Museum and, nearly forty years later, I was a museum curator - with no salary! I think Miss Coe would be pleased!"

JP interviewing Bryen Wood on radio

CORE! THE GOOD LIFE

The Bushey Horticultural Society would be most pleased to hear from you if you know of the location of any Bushey Grove apple tree still in existence!

Research by the Bushey Museum has established that there are two stories concerning the antecedents of the aforementioned apple.

One theory is that a certain Mrs Good *'crossed'* the "*Queen*" and "*Bismarck*" varieties and came up with "*Bushey Grove*". The second theory (and the one I prefer) is that John Thomas Good and his lady wife chanced to purchase an apple from the local shop near Broad Street, (Mr Good was a Chief Clerk at Broad Street Station in the 1890s). He and his wife owned a horticultural nursery in Bushey, they liked the apple they purchased and so they saved the pips and developed the Bushey Grove variety. The Goods also owned land where Bushey Grove Road now is and they had an orchard there, the nursery business prospered and the development of the apple took place in the Bushey Grove orchard, hence Bushey has an apple all of its own. The Good's had four daughters and there are still descendants of the family living in Bushey. The museum showed some of the apples at the Lucy-Kemp Welch Gallery in 1986, they were later made into a pie, oh the Good Life!

A Village At the Crossroads

Dagnall stands on the very borders of the three counties of Beds, Herts and Bucks, in truth it is not an example of a beautiful English village, but it is situated very close to Ashridge and is a good place to start your exploration of the area. The village probably took its name from a Viking chief named Dagga, from the ninth to the eleventh century the Vikings carried out raids on Anglo Saxon England and, for various reasons (some likely to have been of a romantic nature) several of the invaders became absorbed into local life (maybe it wasn't romantic, it could have been that they simply didn't fancy the sea cruise back to their own homeland, it must have been a long row!). We know nothing about Dagga but we do know about a chap named Ulf who died in 1064, he was Lord of Edlesborough (Just down the road) and Studham and Dagnall. Recently the villagers have worked very hard to restore the pond in Dagnall, records indicate that there was a pond on the site in 1297; Sir Henry Sprigurnall, was Lord of the manor and he owned a house close by. There are no known remains of the chapel that once existed in Dagnall but names such as Chapel Lane, Chapel Wick and Chapel Dell can be seen in the village to this day. So, enjoy lunch at the village pubs in Dagnall, Then....

All Saints Church, Dagnall

Ashridge and the Duke

Since I am much fitter than David Spain I could recommend that you walk from Dagnall to Ashridge, but I won't. Leave Dagnall (in your car) and follow the signpost at the crossroads for Berkhamsted and Little Gaddesden. You will immediately thank me for advising you to drive because the hill is long! But enjoy the surrounding countryside as you climb to the peak. Stay on the tree lined lane which will take you past some rather grand houses hidden among the trees. Just as an aside, some of you may remember a music hall act called '*Elsie and Doris Waters*', the sisters lived in Ashridge for many years, and just as another aside (I enjoy the odd aside) Elsie and Doris had a rather famous brother named Jack Warner, he of '*Dixon of Dock Green*' fame as well as many movies. But back to Ashridge. It was Edmund, Earl of Cornwall who ordered a house to be built in the woods at Little Gaddesden, it was to be a monastery for the Grey Monks. The original settlement consisted of some nineteen French monks, and became known as the College of Bonhommes. The later name, Ashridge certainly relates to the Ash tree which, throughout history had religious connotations. The walks through the forest reveal peaceful glades where you can picnic and watch the deer meander through the trees. The Bridgewater Monument is open to the public, '*Spainy*' couldn't manage the stairs so don't expect a photo of the view from the top! Francis Egerton it was who, after he become 3rd Duke of Bridgewater surprised his family by indulging himself in the construction of canals. Such a pastime was considered to be a huge business gamble at the time (1759) but the Duke persisted and became forever associated with canals. In 1796, when the final stretch of the Grand Junction Canal was completed, Francis (or the Duke if you prefer) was said to be earning more than £80,000 per year from the Bridgewater Canal alone, a considerable achievement when you consider that, at one time he had been in debt to the tune of £60, 000.

Management College at Ashridge

Aldbury Pond and Stocks

John O' Gaddesden's house, Little Gaddesden

Bridgewater Monument, Ashridge

PITSTONE - PRUNES AND 'PREACHER PILGRIM'

It was a clear and sunny January morning when historian and writer Vivienne Evans and I met up with David Spain at the village of Pitstone, perfect weather for a walk around the Church of St Mary the Virgin. The church is situated some way from the centre of the village, Vivienne suspects that the reason for this might be that the homes of the workers in the cement industry would have been built close to the factory and the village centre has therefore moved over the years. St Mary the Virgin was founded in 1180 by William De Chendult, Lord of the Manor of Morrants situated in a nearby field. Pitstone has close links with Ashridge and the church was given to Ashridge Monastery in 1379; with the dissolution of the monasteries the church passed to Richard Snowe. Some altar screens were destroyed during the reign of Elizabeth I and the papist paintings were whitewashed over. When we visited work was under way to renovate parts of the church including the walls where the paintings are. The church is closed for regular services and a worthy band of volunteers have worked hard to maintain both the building itself and the area around it. I hate the word redundant but St Mary the Virgin is part of the Redundant Churches Trust, however with the work put in by local people it is still a wonderful place to visit and if all you want to do is sit and take in the view your visit will not be in vain.

There is a great deal to see and enjoy in the immediate area of Pitstone, although many of the original dwellings are long gone, you can visit Pitstone windmill, it is one of the oldest surviving post mills in the country dating back to around 1627. Close by is Brook End Mill and The Mill House, until the first part of the 20th Century they were part of a water mill, granary, stables, dwelling and bakery. The Mill House was sold by one Fred Jellis in 1938 and since then has had a somewhat chequered history, among other things the premises have housed evacuees, been used as a storage for second-hand furniture and by a unit of Irish Guards (prior to the Normandy landings). Records show that during the Second World War children and their mothers, who were evacuated to the area from London, enjoyed their first taste of village life in Pitstone.

Church of St Mary the Virgin, Pitstone

Pitstone Post Mill before restoration, circa 1910

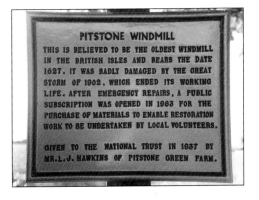

PITSTONE WINDMILL

THIS IS BELIEVED TO BE THE OLDEST WINDMILL IN THE BRITISH ISLES AND BEARS THE DATE 1627. IT WAS BADLY DAMAGED BY THE GREAT STORM OF 1902, WHICH ENDED ITS WORKING LIFE. AFTER EMERGENCY REPAIRS, A PUBLIC SUBSCRIPTION WAS OPENED IN 1963 FOR THE PURCHASE OF MATERIALS TO ENABLE RESTORATION WORK TO BE UNDERTAKEN BY LOCAL VOLUNTEERS.

GIVEN TO THE NATIONAL TRUST IN 1937 BY MR. L. J. HAWKINS OF PITSTONE GREEN FARM.

Restored Mill at Pitstone, 2000

MEN (AND WOMEN) OF STRAW?

So good was the reputation of the straw plaiters of Wigginton in Hertfordshire that the market buyers had no hesitation in climbing the steep hill that leads to the village. Straw plaiting was an essential part of the village economy for just about a hundred years up to the time of the First World War. Doll stuffing and brush making took over between the wars and I visited in the late sixties! My friend Alan Smith lived in Wigginton for a while when he was first married and I often drove my Morris Minor '*pickup*' truck along the lanes from Croxley Green to visit him and his wife Dorothy. Alan and I would enjoy a Colne Spring Ale (only available in the Winter months) at the local while Dorothy and my girlfriend of the time (don't mention this to Mrs '*P*'!) had a bit of a natter. In truth and much as I liked Alan, I had an ulterior motive, the lanes between Croxley Green and Wigginton offered ample opportunity to pull off the road for a '*Brief Encounter*' before I dropped the girlfriend home! Sorry, I digress, Wigginton...... It appears in the Domesday Book as Wigentone and, though it is popular with commuters, it is quite easy to miss the village because it is tucked away at the top of the hill. Lord Rothschild who lived at nearby Tring would send hampers on a covered wagon at Christmas, each one would be labelled with the village children's names, when the snow fell the kids would lay sacks on the road to ensure that the wagon with their Yuletide sweets, nuts oranges and various other '*goodies*' would reach its destination.

Local Straw Plaiters

Footbridge over the A41 bypass, 1994

Lord Rothschild of Tring

The Brewhouse Pub, Wigginton

Wigginton Church

BERKHAMSTED HAS A LOT TO ANSWER FOR!

I was making a recording at the site of the castle in the town with author Scott Hastie when the name David Spain was mentioned. Scott promised to introduce me to his photographer friend and foolishly I agreed, I can't blame Berkhamsted I suppose, but I do feel that Scott could have behaved more responsibly. Nevertheless Berkhamsted has a lot to commend it, not least Ashlyns School.

Artists impression of Berkhamsted Castle at the time of King Edward IV

ASHLYNS SCHOOL AND THE 'CARING CAPTAIN'

Captain Thomas Coram founded his Hospital School in 1739, he had become disillusioned with what he had witnessed on the streets where babies were dying after being abandoned. William Hogarth along with several other painters supported Coram and temporary premises were found in Hatton Garden, sixty children were admitted. In 1742 work began on a new hospital in Bloomsbury, by 1752 there were over six hundred children being cared for. In 1926 the valuable site in London was sold and the school again took up temporary accommodation, between 1933 and 1935 buildings were erected on the site of what is now Ashlyns school, Berkhamsted. Children aged between five and fifteen were admitted to the Hertfordshire school in 1935. The manner in which children were cared for didn't change all that much through the years. Babies were baptised and given a new name so that the mothers identity was protected. So high was the demand for places that staff had to devise a system of balloting. White, red and black balls were placed in a bag, the drawing of a white ball meant that the child was admitted, a red ball denoted a place on a reserve list and a black ball meant that mothers were turned away. In 1836 a parliamentary commission defined the methods of admission: Children had to be illegitimate, unless the father had been a soldier or sailor who had been killed in the service of his country, the child had to be already born and under twelve months old, the mother had to be of a good character *'previous to her misfortune or delivery'* and the father had to have deserted the child or be unable to be found so as to be compelled to maintain the child.

In April 1995 the governors of the school opted for grant maintained status, the work of Thomas Coram's Foundation continues to this day and some callers to the *'Out and About'* programme remember the school children marching with a band to Berkhamsted station at the start of their summer holiday.

You will find a more detailed account of the history of the school, Ashlyns House and the castle in Scott Hastie and David Spain's book *'A Hertfordshire Valley'* published by Alpine Press at Kings Langley.

Thomas Coram was born in Dorset in 1668, his father was a Master mariner and young Thomas went to sea as a cabin boy aged just twelve years, *"I went to sea several years before Charles II died"* he told people on his return from five years at sea. The Coram family moved to Hackney, London and young Thomas became an apprentice shipwright, as he grew up he became a good friend of the rector of St. Botolphs Without, Aldgate and he became Inspector of Cargoes at Liverpool. Aged twenty five, Coram went to Boston, Massachusetts as a shipwright, he made a considerable fortune and was considered a great innovator. On his return to England he moved to Taunton, Devon where he followed a somewhat abortive career in local politics, he returned to the sea and retired in 1721. Described by Robert Walpole as *"the most honest, most disinterested and most knowing about the colonies"* Coram was an expert on the colonies and was a trustee for Georgia. The Prince of Wales contributed twenty guineas towards Coram's one hundred and sixty guineas per annum pension, Coram died in 1751 at his lodgings in Leicester Square, he will forever be associated with Ashlyns.

Ashlyns School, Berkhamsted 2000

HENRY MOORE

Just two miles from the Hertfordshire village of Much Hadham, tucked away along a country lane you will find one of England's greatest art treasures. The seventy acre site at Perry Green was for many years the home of one of the best known sculptors in the world, Henry Moore. The great man was born in Castleford, Yorkshire, he was the seventh of eight children born to coal miner Raymond Moore and his wife Mary. Raymond was the type of father who wanted his children to get the very best out of life and he encouraged young Henry well enough for the boy to achieve a scholarship to a secondary school. Henry began work as a student teacher at his old school in Castleford, he joined the army at the age of eighteen and took part in the battle of Cambrai. Active service for Henry Moore ended when he was gassed and he returned to England.

Back in Yorkshire Henry gained an ex-serviceman's grant and went to Leeds School of Art, so insistent was our Henry that he wanted to study sculpture that the college employed him as an instructor. Henry took a scholarship to the Royal College of Art in London and very soon his career flourished. He met a young painting student named Irina Radetsky and they were married a year later.

Henry Moore's house, Perry Green

Moore's first commission, for a sculpture relief, was for the new London Transport Headquarters in 1928. The comment of one London critic would not have been music to Henry's ears, it went thus: *"The cult of ugliness triumphs at the hands of Mr Moore"*. Notwithstanding this early criticism Moore's career continued on an upward spiral. Moore became a war correspondent at the outbreak of World War Two, he made drawings of people sheltering in the London Underground, these were received with great acclaim. Some of Moore's most famous pieces are on show at Perry Green, it could be said to be one of Hertfordshire's best kept secrets, except that it's not really a secret, it's just that the Perry Green Centre could not cope with masses of people descending upon them at one time. You really need to telephone the centre before you visit, if you do, you will not be disappointed. Moore's studio looks as if the great man had just left it to pop out to the shops and the grounds are filled with his works. Moore purchased several of the buildings in the surrounding area of Perry Green, in fact the only thing that is not owned by the Moore estate in Perry Green is the red telephone kiosk! The Foundation try to keep things as Henry Moore left them when he died in 1986 at the grand old age of 88.

You will find that you are encouraged to touch the sculptures which is most refreshing and quite correct, after all a great work of art should be touched as well as seen, but you can't climb them! Come to think of it, there would be no point in David Spain trying to climb a statue, the last time he tried that was in Trafalgar Square on VE Night!

You must visit Perry Green, telephone: 01279 843333, The Foundation opens its doors between April and October, guided tours start at 2.30pm and last around 90 minutes, but it will take you longer if you choose to spend some time in the grounds.

Three Piece Sculpture: Vertebrae 1968-69

Family Group 1948-49

Abbot's Hill School (Year 10) visit 1999

Two Piece Reclining Figure: Points 1969-70

GREAT OFFLEY - HERTFORDSHIRE, NOT BEDFORDSHIRE!

In his book '*Hertfordshire*' Arthur Jones describes the design of the chancel of St Mary Magdalene in the village of Great Offley as "*seriously out of place*" he does state that it is not "*unpleasing*" to give him his due. I disagree with Mr Jones, and like the monument to Sir Thomas Salisbury and his wife that dominates the south side of the chancel. From the outside St Mary Magdalene is a fairly unsurprising medieval building, it is only when you enter the church that you will find the medieval mixed with the more modern chancel. There is also a Jewish stained glass window, people are not sure just how the window got to be in the church and along with the chancel it serves to make for a rather unusual village church. Because it is situated so close to Luton many people assume that Offley (as it is known locally) is in Bedfordshire, don't let the villagers hear you say so! They are rightly proud of their village and there is still a strong community feel to the place. It is well worth leaving the nearby by-pass to spend a couple of hours wandering around Offley, there are a number of Georgian houses, a couple of good pubs and of course Offley Place. This was built in the 17th century for Sir Richard Spencer and is now used as a conference centre owned by Hertfordshire County Council. Villagers remember with affection the broadcaster Brian Johnston who spent some of his childhood in the village. What a wonderful fellow Mr Johnston was, I was privileged to meet him on a couple of occasions he was the epitome of an English gent. On the Saturday of the cricket test at his beloved Lords, Brian would always wear what he called his co-respondent shoes, white and brown brogues. Always willing to stop for a chat '*Johners*' recognised that he was a lucky man to be able to travel the world reporting on cricket. Johnston will always be remembered for his '*Down Your Way*' radio series when he would visit villages and towns across the length and breadth of the land interviewing the real people, naturally we talked about '*Down Your Way*' when we met and I suppose it was Brian as much, as anyone, who convinced me that so called '*ordinary folk*' have much more to say than many of the big names.

St. Mary Magdelene Church at Offley

Mick Collins, Landlord of The Red Lion

T.W. Butchers, Offley

Offley Place

The Green Man

Return of the bells after refurbishment at Offley Church

Biggleswade (Bedfordshire) to Battersea and Back.

One afternoon in the early summer of 1860 a certain Mrs Tealby visited a friend, Mrs Major in Islington. Instead of taking afternoon tea, Mrs Major took her friend down to the kitchen where a pathetic little dog lay in front of the kitchen range, the poor thing was in the last stages of starvation. Mrs Major had come across the dog when out for a walk earlier in the day and, filled with pity she had brought it home to try and nurse it back to health. Mrs Tealby offered her help, and within days the two ladies had rescued several other stray dogs from the streets.

Our Mrs Tealby was the more forceful of the two ladies and quickly decided to try to do something for more of the waifs and strays of London's streets. She persuaded her brother to help, he approached a number of acquaintances to get involved and on October 2nd they published their first prospectus for their dogs home. They appealed for funds for the *Temporary Home for Lost and Starving Dogs*'. The first committee meeting was held in November 1860 at the offices of the RSPCA in Pall Mall. Mary Tealby found a stableyard in Holloway and many more dogs came through the doors. The home's first member of staff was one James Pavitt and he registered each dog by giving them a name and a number attached to a disc on its collar. This system exists to this very day and of course the home we are talking of is Battersea Dogs Home. The home received a bad press when it was first opened - not surprising when you think that starving women and children living on the streets of the capital was a common sight in Victorian England. Charles Dickens published an article in 1862, in the piece he compared what he had seen at The Two Dogs Show (a forerunner of Crufts) to what he had witnessed at The Temporary Home for Lost and Starving Dogs and through Dickens support and that of others, attitudes soon began to change.

Mary Tealby died of cancer in 1865 aged 64, but not before she was able to see the fruits of her labours, the beginnings of one of London's most famous institutions. In 1871 the home moved to its present site in Battersea and was renamed The Dogs' Home Battersea.

Very little is known about Mrs Tealby, she was evidently the estranged wife of a timber merchant from Hull. For the last few years of her life she lived in a small house in Islington with her brother, the Reverend Edward Bates. He was the one time incumbent at St Andrews Church, Biggleswade, where they are both buried. Recently representatives of Battersea visited the grave to place flowers there and tidy it.

St. Andrews, Biggleswade

The grave of Mrs Tealby 1801-1865

St. Andrews, Biggleswade

Walter Justis was the first Vicar of the church, he was instituted in 1276. In his time the church consisted of the south aisle, it still has its original roof of English oak with bosses and angels (some angels are missing, they were sold to Cockayne Hatley church in the 18th century). Hugh Frankelyn was succeeded by Robert De Clifton in 1349, a significant date because it was the year of the Black Death. Half the population of Bedfordshire died in the plague. The death rate among the clergy was particularly high and a change of incumbent is a common feature in churches.

The Great Fire

A couple of hundred years ago Biggleswade was a busy market town situated on the Great North Road. The town had many Inns and would have been a convenient place for coaches and other travellers to stop. At '*The Crown*' on June 16th, 1785 a servant was raking out the hot ashes from the fire in the kitchen, he deposited them in the yard close to some straw which caught fire, someone quickly filled two leather buckets from the pump in the yard and that, as they say should have been that. Such is the way of things that a mad dog is said to have rushed through the yard at the precise moment the man with the buckets was making for the fire, so what should have been a small conflagration resulted in the Great Fire of Biggleswade. The fire took hold and the wood and thatch buildings fed the thirsty flames. Quickly the blaze spread across the road, '*The Swan*' was next to fall victim, men working in the fields rushed to help the townsfolk. People from Stratton, Home, Langford and other villages gave assistance. After some four hours the blaze was under control but not before nearly a third of the town had been destroyed. Over four hundred people were "*totally deprived of sustenance and must have perished had it not been for the charitable relief of those who escaped and the liberal contributions of the neighbourhood*". Though many of the poorer people were not insured, Biggleswade seems to have recovered quite quickly.

The site of the Great Fire at Biggleswade in 1785

THE LAST REMAINING PEAR TREE AND A GHOST

My friend Bernard West (as you will know if you read 'Out and About' volume one!) is, among other things fascinated by matters archaeological. I telephoned Bernard one day and suggested I should buy him lunch and a drink, since he isn't all that interested in drink (oh really!) he agreed. I offered to drive and duly collected my friend from his delightful home in the village of Willington close to Bedford. Now when you offer to take Bernard for a drive you should prepare yourself for a history lesson, it doesn't matter where you go, he will have some interesting snippet of information for you. Mr West directed me to take the back lanes to Old Warden so I did. *"If you care to slow down a little John"* suggested my friend *"There's a tree on this stretch of road that might be of interest, you will have heard of the famous Warden Abbey and the pear that bears its name, well (pointing vaguely out of the car window) there is the last remaining tree"*. Not content with a little horticultural history, Bernard implored me to drive even slower as he pointed out the line of a Roman Road, he really is a great person to go out to lunch with.

Over lunch itself Bernard explained how, many years ago he and his wife were involved on an archaeological dig on the site of Warden Abbey close to Bedford. There isn't much of the building remaining now but you can (I believe) arrange to rent it for a weekend break, if you do, you should hear Bernard's story first. The archaeologists found several skeletons on the abbey site and one of Bernard's jobs was to lay them out in the building for safe keeping over night. Bernard swears that for several mornings running he would unlock the building to find the skeletons had moved during the night! Exasperated by this he shouted very loudly to inform the perpetrators that the skeletons would all be laid to rest properly in the fullness of time. At this moment Mr West pushed aside his pudding plate which had, once contained a delightful spotted dick and told me "do you know John from that time the skeletons remained exactly as I had left them". Bernard West is a great chap and a wonderful storyteller.

JP interviewing Bernard West (on right)

The remains of Warden Abbey

EVERSHOLT AND A LOVABLE LLAMA

It can be a little confusing if you have an appointment in the village of Eversholt. It's not that the village is difficult to find, in fact it's only a few short miles along the Bedfordshire lanes from Flitwick. I left home in good time for my appointment and asked for directions in a garage and then got stuck behind a line of vintage cars! Trust me to visit Eversholt on the only day in the year when '*old car enthusiasts*' decided to hold a rally and furthermore picked a route taking in Eversholt. It has to be said that one can understand them wanting to visit this part of Bedfordshire. Woburn Abbey is nearby, much of the land would have been part of the Duke's estate at one time and he knew a good thing when he saw it. It is yet another part of the county that proves how wrong people can be when they tell you Bedfordshire is flat and boring. The really confusing thing about Eversholt is the fact that it is made up of about fourteen '*Ends*'. Originally the '*Ends*' would have been simply one farmhouse or a cottage or two, these days they form the village. Witts End (which is where I appropriately found myself) is said to be a corruption of '*Whites*' and Church End is obvious, as is Brooks End and Hills End, though I have no idea how Higher Rads End gained its name. Since I required Church End I resolved to keep my eyes open for a church spire, it didn't work but I was lucky enough to stumble upon the fine house known as Church Farm, (after visiting several other Ends). Paul Jay owns Church Farm and a most pleasant character he is. I was offered a cup of coffee in the spacious kitchen and took some time to admire the amazing array of bric a brac, pictures, photographs and collectables Paul has put together over the years. One room contains probably one of the largest collections of drawings, paintings and photographs of Llamas in this country! Not surprising when you learn that it was the Llamas I had come to see.

I fell in love with Brigitte the moment she allowed me to cuddle her, it is true that she is a trifle smelly and maybe her coat is just a little shaggy and OK, so she has been known to spit on occasions! Nevertheless Brigitte is the girl for me. Llamas communicate mainly through body language and once you know what to look for they are quite easy to understand. Paul has around thirty of the animals, 'Russell' was just a week old when I visited and his mum and dad were clearly very proud of him, though Paul did say that 'Blitzen' (dad) would change his attitude towards his son within a year (Blitzen is the only other male and will protect his 'rights'). The Jay's saw an advert in 'Exchange and Mart' and purchased their first Llamas without knowing much about them but they have delved into the history of the animals and love them as much as you love your dog or cat. With long slender necks and what looks like eye make up, I found them entrancing. The Llama is primarily a pack animal but in Bolivia, Peru, Ecuador, Chile and Argentina the Indians have found them to be a source of food and wool as well as using their dried dung for fuel. So Llamas are both useful and beautiful, you might like to know that they are a member of the camel family and that their Latin name is Lama glama (unlike Paul Jay who is known as a Llama Farmer!).

Paul Jay (Llama Farmer), Brigitte & JP

Blitzen, the dominant male Llama

When he is not caring for his Llamas, Paul Jay tends to the needs of his Wallabies! He says that he bought the Wallabies because people thought he was daft to keep Llamas. And when Paul is not tending the Wallabies he restores and races vintage racing cars. David Spain and I were invited into Paul's workshop to take a look.

'Spainy was delighted to find a number plate with 'DS' on it but naturally because the car had been built for a sporting type 'Spainy' had as much trouble climbing into it as he had the Cessna Aircraft at Panshangar (and the hollow tree at Cuffley)'.

Spainy 'stuck again'

Alta racing car 1938

Maserati T26 racing car, 1926

A smug JP knows he can fit in the car!

JP interviews PJ in the workshop

Eversholt Church

The Village Hall, Eversholt

The old cricket pavilion

Skating on Thin Ice at Leighton Buzzard (or Should That be Heath and Reach?)

Over the years several stories about people falling through ice and drowning have come up on the programme. Skating appears to have been a popular pastime in the thirties and forties.

Bob Bates of Leighton Buzzard told me about how his farmer father used to flood one of his fields and charge people who wanted to skate. Bob went on to say that his dad made him try it out first! (Of course, David Spain has been skating on thin ice for years!).

Four generations of the Bates' family lived at Grange Mill, Heath and Reach, Bob was born there in 1928. Bob tells how, as a boy he worked on the farm attached to the mill. Naturally they used horses for almost every task on the farm but in 1938 tractors came along and ploughing was carried out through the day and (provided there was a full moon), at night as well. The tractors had no lights. A year later a local contractor who owned tractors employed a certain Mr Capp to drive one of them. Now Mr Capp had never driven a tractor before so, his employer took the tractor and his new employee to a field of some 28 acres, fixed a chain harrow to the back of the tractor and invited Mr Capp to take his position at the wheel, Mr Capp did so not forgetting to place his lunch box beside him. Mr Evans stayed on the tractor for the first fifty yards and then jumped off leaving a somewhat bemused Mr Capp to get on with it. Satisfied that our hero would cope Mr Evans went to get on with his own work. Seven hours later the contractor returned to find Mr Capp still going round and round! It seems that he hadn't been told how to stop the machine! But he had eaten his lunch!

Tractors ran on TVO in those days and farmers used to rub some of the smelly substance on the peaks of their caps to keep the Gadflies away.

Grange Mill, Heath and Reach, near Leighton Buzzard

View of water wheel

Bob Bates haymaking in 1948

I told you that young Bob used to skate on the frozen fields didn't I? Well it wasn't quite as simple as that, much preparation went into providing the surface. When he judged the weather to be right Bob's dad would flood a five acre meadow and wait for about three days of frost and it was, then that he invited his son to try it out! Bates senior would then place a board in Bardells Fish and Chip shop in Leighton Buzzard advertising *'Skating at Grange Mill'*. Another board would be placed with Thrody Brothers, Luton and as many as a thousand people would turn up to skate on the meadow. At night the people parked cars with their headlights on all around the meadow to enable the skaters to see who they were bumping into! Bob says that a local *'Well to do'* lady would bring her five children but because the charge for skating was sixpence each, she would say *"Just one skating please"*. Some people who were poor skaters would bring a dining room chair with them and toddle across the ice holding the chair in front of them, young Bob, being a good skater enjoyed whizzing past and whipping the chair away, he hasn't changed much over the years! On one occasion a local *'gent'* who had spent the night in The Swan Hotel came to the meadow with his car, he drove onto the ice scattering the skaters left, right and centre. Mr Bates asked him to stop, but he refused, so the farmer went to the farm and came back with a pickaxe, he broke the ice surrounding the car and the vehicle sunk! It stayed there for six weeks until the ice melted.

Bob Bates is a real character, still going strong at the age of seventy three, he recalls swimming in the river in the Summer months, he and his friends would wear those old woollen swimsuits. The boys did put up a makeshift canopy where the girls could change, but it didn't stop the lads taking a peak!

When the war started evacuees came to Heath and Reach from Kentish Town, Bob remembers that they couldn't stop eating Blackberries and then being off school for three days with the *'trots'*. The Local Defence Volunteers were another source of amusement Bob tells the following story:

"After Dunkirk the threat of invasion grew and the LDV arrived one Saturday morning, they told my father that they were going to dig some trenches beside the river so that if the Germans came, they could stand in the trenches and throw petrol bombs at the tanks. Dad tried to warn them, but they wouldn't listen, they dug their trenches and then returned on Sunday morning, in the dark to practise. The brave lads jumped into the trenches which had filled with water overnight!

Mr Stevens used to deliver the milk in the village and as I came home from school in the evening I would creep along the outside of the old, black tarred cowshed where Mr Stevens was milking the cows, I would wait until I was level with him and then kick the boards as hard as I could, he never caught us.

A man by the name of Twydle was a bit of an odd job man and poacher. One day, when I was about ten years old, I smuggled my dad's gun out of the house, I shot a rabbit close to the hedge and some of the shot hit Mr Twydle who was cycling up the lane. The shot bedded itself in the poachers moleskin trousers and he was unhurt, we agreed that if I gave him the rabbit, he wouldn't tell my dad! After the war my dad purchased a tractor, my first job was to mow the grass, so off I went on the tractor with dad following behind like when we used horses, slowly I opened the throttle until dad was trotting behind me, then running, after a while he gave up and went home. He told my mum that I had done it on purpose, it wasn't my fault, dad kept shouting 'whoa back' at the tractor!"

Bob Bates revels in the memories of his childhood, he told me about an incident that he couldn't dream of repeating:
"In the early fifties I was trying out an old Webley air gun, we were down by the river. Close by was an old dung loader with a hydraulic frame, there was a hollow cross member on the frame. My mate bet me that I couldn't put a shot through the hollow pipe, I was a pretty good shot and managed it at the first attempt, unfortunately the pipe was in line with our kitchen window. The pellet went through the frame, over the garden and through the window, it hit the newspaper my dad was reading! Couldn't do it again if I tried!"

CLOPHILL - CAINHOE CASTLE - FLITTON

I pass the village of Clophill every day of my working life and I always find myself wondering what it would have been like in days gone by. You can still see the outline of Cainhoe Castle, sheep and cattle graze on the spot where Nigel d' Albini a Norman knight fortified the hilltop. The original bailey was dug into an ancient quarry. The face of the area is even today in a stage of transition, Fullers Earth is being quarried and new lakes formed as the work continues. Close by are the remains of a medieval village where the Black Death of 1348 brought about the death of Peter de St Croix and his son Robert as well as most of the villagers. This is probably the reason the village was deserted and Clophill grew up just down the road. Despite the fact that the busy A6 road runs through Clophill it is a most pleasant village, there was a straw plaiting factory in the High Street and the ladies would take their plait to the Flying Horse pub where a carrier would collect it for transport to Luton.

The Clophill Charity came about through a somewhat bizarre set of circumstances. One Thomas Dearman worked in one of the large houses in the area and it is said that his mother called on him to beg for help. Dearman turned his mother away but on his death it was found that he had left all his money to the poor of the village. Knives Lane is where animals where taken to be slaughtered and The Slade is where people who had misbehaved in the nearby village of Silsoe were banished!

Outline of Cainhoe Castle

Clophill Village Green

JP and Spainy's photo assistant Natalie (inset) by the village lock-up

FLITTON AND THE DE GREY MAUSOLEUM

Just a short journey from Clophill is the village of Flitton, the parish church is 15thC and built of local brown sandstone. The address of the church keyholder is on a board outside the church, take the time to get the key because you should not miss the De Grey Mausoleum. It is the burial place of the De Grey family of Wrest Park, Silsoe. Work was in started in 1614, the earliest monument is the brass to Henry Grey. The reclining figures of another Henry, the fifth Earl of Kent and his wife are carved in alabaster and brightly painted. When you first see the mausoleum it will be through a locked iron door and you get the impression that only the fifth Earl and his wife are within, but! Unlock the iron door and you will gain access to three or four other galleries where the lives of other members of the family can be seen. It really is stunning, all the more so because you simply don't expect to see such monuments in a small village church.

Vivienne Evans & JP in the mausoleum

The keys are available from:

Mrs Stimpson,
3, Highfield Road, Flitton.
Telephone: 01525 860094

The De Grey family house of Wrest Park, Silsoe

COACHES, CARRIAGES AND GARDENS

When people tell you that Luton has very little to offer, don't believe them, there is plenty to do for young and old alike. Wardown Park has its lake and gardens to wander through and then there is the town's museum tucked away in the park. The museum began its life as the home of Frank Scargill, a solicitor. During the Great War the house became a convalescent home for servicemen and quite recently a folded service cap was found in the roof when repairs were being made. Whether you are a '*Lutonian*' or not you will enjoy a visit to the museum.

MOSSMAN COLLECTION AND STOCKWOOD PARK

George Mossman of Caddington began his working life with Panter's the butchers of Luton, young George enjoyed working with the horses that pulled the delivery vans. His interest in horses and the vehicles they pulled was to remain with him for the rest of his life. Mossman became a successful farmer and businessman and his success enabled him to build a fantastic collection of horse-drawn vehicles. After the Second World War the spread of cars, lorries and tractors saw the demise of the horse as a means of transport and many horse-drawn vehicles were tucked away in barns and out buildings. Mossman sought these vehicles out and often purchased them very cheaply. At the farm in Caddington, George employed coach builders and other craftsmen, they refurbished the vehicles and put them into a roadworthy condition. George Mossman became a familiar figure in Luton and South Bedfordshire during the 1950's, his carriages were used for weddings, shows and special events. Assisted by his daughters Patricia and Christine, Mossman built up a reputation as an expert. He financed his passion from his other business interests and many famous people came to him for advice, one such a person was the industrialist Calouste Gulbenkian (odd how the name Gulbenkian occurs in stories in this book!). Over the years the cinema and TV industry used Mossman's coaches and carriages in their productions and George appeared on the screen many times as a '*stand in*' driver. When a particular vehicle was required for a film it was George's expertise that was sought, he ensured that they were historically accurate.

In 1988 Mossman organised a drive from London to Brighton to commemorate the centenary of James Selby's record breaking journey. Selby had completed the trip in eight hours and, looking at the coach which is now in the Mossman Collection, I can only marvel at his resilience! Selby's coach, '*Old Times*' is probably the most famous to survive from the heyday of coaching. From Phaeton's to chariots, Springless State Waggons to farm vehicles, gigs and even Dr Zhivago's sled, find them all at the Mossman Collection in Stockwood Park.

Telephone: 01582 738714 for details

Examples of the types of carriages to be found in the Mossman Collection at Stockwood Park

STOCKWOOD PARK - THE GARDENS - THE CRAFT MUSEUM

It will take you a full day to visit the Mossman Collection, the Craft Museum and the Period Gardens at Stockwood. The gardens cover over nine centuries of English garden history and they are an absolute delight. The Hamilton Finlay Sculpture Garden offers the chance to see the artists work in a natural setting and the Craft Museum will help to brush up your knowledge of rural life. Don't listen when they tell you Luton has little to offer the discerning visitor, because in the first place it has and in the second place, YOU ARE A DISCERNING VISITOR!

EMMA - SCHOOLTEACHER, BROADCASTER AND HEAD PATTER!

To loyal listeners of her Sunday gardening programme Emma Pilgrim is pleasant, charming and intelligent. To the children she teaches at various schools across Beds, Herts and Bucks I am sure that she is friendly, supportive and protective. To me she is the daughter who walks through the front door, pats me on the head and makes straight for the fridge. My middle daughter has been a secretary, HGV driver (with the RAF) and, when we ran a pub, a reluctant waitress. Her mother and myself were very proud the day we stood on a cold and windy airfield at RAF Swinderby for Emma's passing out parade. It was, naturally, a tearful occasion because yet another of our offspring had flown the nest. Mum and I agreed that a spell in the armed forces would do our daughter no harm at all, but we were just a little surprised that she had completed her training. You see, the idea of Emma scrambling through mud soaked ditches with a full combat pack on her back and a gun in her hand was just too much to imagine. Emma is probably the most '*clean conscious*' person I know, even the dog and the cat run when Emma gets a vacuum cleaner in her hand. She takes after her mother when it comes to handing out the orders and she isn't that far behind Mrs '*P*' when it comes to finding jobs for other people (usually dad) around the house. Having decided that life in the armed forces was not for her, my daughter decided to go to university! I was surprised yet again because she had never really shown a lot of interest in education when she was at school (here she takes after dear old dad). Having gained her degree, Emma became a teacher but, being a Pilgrim that was not enough, so she became a broadcaster as well. It's easy really, all you do is work away in the evenings, setting up things for your Sunday programme, (pinch a couple of ideas from dad along the way) and Bingo! You have fabulous broadcasting figures. I am not bitter of course (in fact I am very proud) even though she will insist on patting me on the head!

Emma Pilgrim invites Susie Spain to her radio show

WHATEVER THE SUBJECT

It really doesn't seem to matter what the subject is, if you ask people to telephone, someone will oblige and very often the stories are amusing or moving, never dull:

Pat in Chesham: (When asked about pen pals)

"I was eighteen years old when my brother asked me to become a pen friend to a chap in Africa, his name was Pat Ewodage and he was serving in the Army Pay Corp. Me being carefree, adventurous (and almost grown up!) I agreed, my parents were liberal minded and in any case I didn't ask them!

When Pat's first letter came accompanied with a photograph I realised that he was African, which (in those days) was rather a shock (In 1942/43 white girls and coloured chaps didn't mix).

All of Pat's letters began 'My dearest Patricia, When I receive your letters my heart opens like a flower' and then went on to tell me about his life in Africa. According to him he was engaged to a tribal king's daughter whom he would marry when the war was over.

What amazed me and my parents was the arrival of a coconut through the post. It was shaved of bristles and painted white and addressed in black paint. I still have no idea how he managed to send me such an item in wartime!

Pat also sent me cushion covers made of leather squares, red, black and tan with one square covered with the hair from the mane of a lion. When my future husband suggested that I should stop writing to Pat I did, it was only your programme about such memories that reminded me of this episode in my life".

Pat in Chesham during WW II

St. Mary's, Chesham 2000

The High Street, Chesham

CHALFONT ST PETER - THE HANGING JUDGE AND A POET

Brian Saunders is a regular listener to 'Out and About' and he often telephones to read one of his poems or make a comment about the village where he was born. I made a visit to Brian's home one morning before my programme, it's quite a drive across country from where I live but it was worth it. First up we chatted about the village Brian had known as a child and how he became interested in local history and poetry. Brian is a good storyteller and his memories are all the more relevant because they come from a different perspective - he lost his sight when he was in his early twenties. He was aware that his sight would deteriorate because of a long standing eye problem in the family and did not allow this to deter him from leading a full life. Brian happily relates stories of his childhood when he would ride the army lorries with American soldiers during the second World War or of paddling in the River Misbourne attempting to catch minnows. Because Brian's life is dominated by what he can hear rather than what he can see, he notices the increase in traffic through the village more than most. The Misbourne is not the river it once was and although the village has retained much of its charm, the population has exploded over the years.

The stagecoach which once stood outside The Greyhound Inn (something I remember from my youth) has sadly gone, the inn itself was a staging post in the 18th and early 19th centuries. The notorious Judge Jeffreys lived at The Grange and is known to have held court in the village.

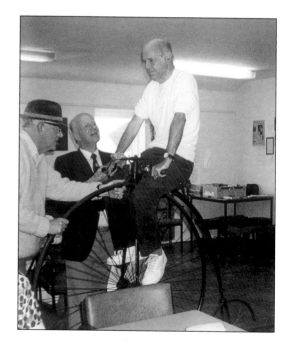

Brian Saunders

BRIAN SAUNDERS - A POEM OR TWO

Working with his amazing Braille typing machine Brian taps out poetry, sometimes funny and sometimes moving, I have selected two of my favourites;

"I ENJOY IT"

I really do enjoy it,
Yes, I really do,
Several times a day at least,
Believe me folks it's true.

I've enjoyed it in the morning,
Laying in my bed,
And I've enjoyed it more than once,
In my potting shed.

I've enjoyed it in the garden,
And on a train as well,
And I've enjoyed it in the bath,
I hope that you won't tell.

Sometimes in the afternoon,
I enjoy it now and then,
And when I've had my tea at six,
I enjoy it once again.

And when I've had my supper,
The wife she says to me,
"Would you like it now my love"
ANOTHER CUP OF TEA!

"IF ONLY"

If only my eyes could see the world
What a wonderful thing it would be,
To go anywhere, and do anything,
And from my white cane I would
be free

If only I could see the faces,
Of the people every day,
But all I hear is the sound of
their feet,
As they pass by on their way.

If only I could see the flowers,
I grow with tender care,
But some of them make perfume,
So I know that they are there.

If only I could see a rainbow,
The stars in the sky at night,
The beauty of the sunset,
It must be a wonderful sight.

If only I could see the colours,
Of Summer, Autumn and Spring,
The yellow beak of the blackbird,
As he throws back his head to sing.

If only I had my life again,
With eyes so clear and bright,
Just close your eyes for a minute,
It's a strange world without any sight.

HIGH WYCOMBE AND 'DIZZY'

Benjamin Disraeli fought several elections in High Wycombe and lived at nearby Hughenden Manor. *"Benjamin married me for my money but if he had the chance again he would marry me for love"* So said *'Dizzy's'* wife when the great man teased her that he had married her for her worldly goods, the lady was probably correct, nevertheless she did come from a wealthy family having an income of some four thousand pounds a year. Disraeli decided on a life in politics in 1871 and sought a seat near Wycombe where his family had settled. He fought and lost three times and decided that he needed to join one of the political parties (previously he sought election as an independent radical). *'Dizzy'* led a somewhat extravagant lifestyle and built up considerable debts as well as a dubious reputation for an affair with the wife of one Sir Francis Sykes. In 1835 he stood as the candidate for Taunton and lost. In 1837 (as a Conservative) Disraeli won the seat for Maidstone in Kent. His maiden speech in the House of Commons did not go down well, he tended to use three words where one would do and his fellow MPs did not care for his rather foppish dress. They tried to shout him down but *'Dizzy'* insisted on finishing his speech with the words *"I will sit down now, but the time will come when you will hear me"*. He married Mrs Wyndham Lewis in 1839 and despite his jocular comments about her wealth they became a devoted couple.

Beech trees abound in the woods surrounding High Wycombe and it is no surprise that furniture making became the traditional industry in the area. Men worked in huts in the beech woods, the trees were felled, their trunks and larger branches cut into manageable lengths, then split into pieces ready for *'turning'*. The *'bodgers'* as they were called, made only the turned parts on simple *'pole lathes'* and sent them off to be assembled into chairs. Because they used these simple methods (no power costs for example) they were able to compete with powered workshops for a long time.

WEST WYCOMBE - CAVES AND A POET'S HEART AND HALF A SWEET!

The village is probably best known for the 'Hellfire Caves' owned by the Dashwood family. The West Wycombe Estate was purchased by the Dashwood family in 1698. In the 18th century the second Baronet began rebuilding the family home, he also rebuilt and enlarged the parish church. The tower is topped with a Golden Ball thought to be a copy of the one in Venice (to be found on the Custom's Building, should you visit Venice).

The caves came about when the site was excavated to provide chalk foundations for a nearby road. These days the caves contain tableaux showing Dashwood and his friends as members of the Hellfire Club as well as other 'well knowns' such as Benjamin Franklin. The Mausoleum was erected in 1765 and mainly commemorates Dashwood's wife. The heart of the well known poet, Paul Whitehead is also buried there.

Visit the caves and the Mausoleum but don't forget to take in the village and the surrounding countryside, there is plenty to see in this beautiful corner of Buckinghamshire. In "The Buckinghamshire Village Book" published by the Women's Institute there is a lovely story from a lady who recalls visiting the village shop owned by one Katy Rippington. It seems that Ms. Rippington would cut a sweet in half rather than give over weight!

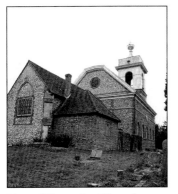
West Wycombe Church

Village of West Wycombe, 2000

Scenic view of West Wycombe Church

Entrance to 'Hellfire Caves'

BUCKINGHAM, STOWE AND CLIFF'S STORY

'The land of Bucca's people in the bend of the river' is a bit of a mouthful so they shortened it to Buckingham, very sensible. It's likely that there was some form of encampment on the River Ouse in Saxon times and the position made it a good place to build a castle. After

the Danes had been beaten off, the need for a castle decreased and in the Domesday Book we find that Aylesbury and other towns became more important to the detriment of Buckingham; when the Assizes were moved to Aylesbury in the 1600's the town's position was again usurped. In 1554 Sir Peter Temple took out a lease on some land at Stowe, just outside Buckingham, then his son Sir John Temple bought the lease in 1591 and the Temple family became very wealthy by enclosing the estate. The Temples fortunes increased when they acquired sugar plantations in the West Indies (and, it has to be said by some pretty well arranged marriages). Sir Thomas Temple purchased the freehold of the manor of Buckingham in 1604 and the family prospered. Another name entered the story when the Grenvilles saw fit to purchase land in the area in the 1800's, this was to ensure that they held political influence in Parliament.

THE GREAT FIRE OF BUCKINGHAM

It was March 1724 or 1725 (depending on which records you take a look at) that the Unicorn Inn close to the Market Square burst into flames, Buckingham's houses were built mainly of timber and lath and plaster and the fire soon spread. Over five hundred people were made homeless.

It seems that, despite the efforts of several characters throughout the centuries, Buckingham was not destined to become the premier town of the county. Nevertheless it has a great deal to commend it. David Spain and I paid a visit to the town, Stowe House and Cliff.

Buckingham 'Town Gaol'

Stowe School, House and Estate, 2000

'ELLO, 'ELLO, 'ELLO - "CLIFF'S IN BUCKINGHAM"

Cliff Smith and his wife Olive live in Buckingham and for many years Cliff was a local 'bobby', one of the old school. When I visited their home Cliff and Olive made me most welcome, I can still taste the Welsh Cakes now. In the days when Cliff administered his 'beat' the Police had no immediate contact with HQ and often had to make pre-arranged calls from the village telephone box. When Cliff fell from his 'Heartbeat like' motorcycle he had to explain First Aid to the passer by who found him. Sitting in his well trimmed garden 'PC Smith' explained how he was responsible for investigating crime, supervised sheep dipping, examined cattle for Warble Fly, stood on duty at farms where animals had Foot and Mouth disease among other things!

The local Police house was very much at the heart of village life, Cliff recalled the time he heard someone enter the house just as he was preparing to take a bit of a rest, a voice called out "I say Cliff have you heard that someone has shot the Vicar of Chearsley", his visitor was The Lord Lieutenant of the county and the weapon used was an air gun and the Vicar had not been hit. It was a requirement of the job that the constable should know most, if not all of the local criminals. Having come off duty at 6 am. one morning Cliff's sleep was interrupted by a villager holding a pigeon. The man explained that he had found the bird and asked our Cliff what he should do with it, Cliff had little difficulty in telling him!

On another occasion (and at 3 am in the morning) Cliff received a call from a lady who was in a nearby telephone kiosk, she had been kicked out by her husband and demanded Cliff should return her to bed immediately.

Speeding through the villages is not a new thing, one man who was caught by Cliff explained to the magistrates, "I saw the Policeman on his motorcycle coming up behind me, I thought he wanted a 'burn up' so I accelerated to show him just how fast my motorbike was". The villages that Cliff covered were home to several well known people and one Sunday afternoon he was assisted by a very 'well to do' lady. He was patrolling the country lanes on his motorcycle when he came upon a group of youths, they were all carrying guns and so Cliff searched them, he found two pheasants stuffed inside their coats, the birds were full of shotgun pellets but the young men insisted that their dogs had caught the birds. When Cliff commented that the dogs must be 'damn good shots' the youngsters admitted to lying. Our hero had little idea exactly how he was going to take the youths into custody as well as carrying the evidence back to the police station, help was at hand! A Rolls Royce appeared and was duly flagged down. The driver of the 'Roller' was non other than Mrs Gulbenkian, wife of oil magnate Nubar Gulbenkian, she kindly agreed to carry the evidence to Cliff's house.

Cliff and Olive attended a local 'Barn Dance' soon after being posted to Buckingham. A group of local lads approached Cliff and he told Olive to expect trouble, this particular group had been arrested by Cliff on several occasions, they had threatened to 'work him over' if they came across him in civvies. Cliff prepared himself for trouble, the lads came up to him and one of them said "Nice to have you in our village Mr Smith, can we buy you a drink!".

Mrs Gulbenkian

I like the story about a man who once knocked on the door of the Police house and asked Cliff if he knew of any local uninhabited farms, he wanted to find such a building he said, because the BBC required one for a film they were making. Cliff couldn't help and the fellow walked off, some months later the Great Train Robbery happened and Cliff saw his visitor's face on the wanted posters!

Cliff recognises that without Olive his life as a village policeman would have been doubly difficult, I recognise that a visit to their home would be less enjoyable without Olive's Welsh Cakes.

Cliff Smith (ex-policeman) with his wife Olive

ADELAIDE IN AYLESBURY - HER STORY

Adelaide is a regular caller to my radio programme and a lovely lady with a beautiful speaking voice. During the course of our conversations it became clear that she had a story to tell and I managed to convince her to write it for me:

"I was born in Georgetown, British Guiana which is now called the Republic of Guyana. We were a poor family but I never ever heard my mum complain or get upset about anything, she simply got on with life. There was always fresh bread and cakes, the smell was divine. Mum also made her own drinks, mauby, ginger beer and others, she was always cooking. I can remember her working very hard, she never went out to work.

I remember someone from around the corner making clothes, fabric was only twelve cents a yard. We were always smartly dressed for our visit to Sunday School and on our return off came our Sunday clothes. We would have treats like home made ice cream, cakes and drinks it was wonderful. Vegetable and beef or cowheel soup was our Sunday lunch".

Although Adelaide's family were poor her early life sounds somewhat idyllic but things changed when her mother died on December 3rd 1942, Adelaide writes:

"I was her third child as far as I can remember, I was eight years old. We all lived with our dad, I cannot remember any other relatives like aunts or uncles or even grandparents. I attended a Catholic school and was well looked after for a short while. One day my world came crashing down around my ears. My dad told us that he had found a home for us girls, the boys would remain with him. Dad said that the family we would live with were cousins of his. When the time came for us to leave our home we packed together what little we had and travelled by bus into the unknown, I can vaguely recall dad kissing us goodbye before he left us with this strange family. My eldest sister was twelve at the time and my younger four years old. Days went by and we were fed when the family felt like feeding us, I had never experienced such hunger when my mum was alive. One thing I remember well is us having to take care of ourselves, some things I cannot mention, they are best forgotten. Our dad never came to visit us and my older sister did not hang around too long, she ran away to live with friends and I, in turn had to look after my little sister. When I was about eight and half years old I was sent to work for a family who had children. I worked two hours before going to school and two after school. I did the cleaning and cleared up after the children who were not even potty trained, can you imagine me having to look after other children? I was only a child myself!

Adelaide's father got to hear what was happening to her and her sister and came to take them home. By this time Adelaide was nine and a half years old, she had to get herself and her sister ready for school, her brothers looked after themselves and her father was out to work all day and the kids were left to their own devices:

"Here I was on my way home from school doing the shopping and preparing the evening meal, cleaning the house, getting our clothes ready for school and doing the laundry. Talk about a child having to carry a burden, that was me. Eventually dad found another family to foster me and my sister, this time closer to where he lived. The cruelty started all over again, one step out of line and I was beaten, my sister was spared the torture because of her age. My job at nights was to care for my foster mother's kids, she had three boys. If the boys awoke during the night their mother would wake me to change their nappies, feed them and get them back to sleep, my, my what a life! I had to get out of bed early to prepare the breakfast for everyone, run errands, do the shopping and whatever else there was to be done. By the time I got to school I was exhausted and often fell asleep at my desk, when this happened the teacher woke me by caning me across my back.

What a tremendous spirit little Adelaide must have had, learning to survive at such a young age and learn to survive she did:

"One night I had enough of the eldest boy crying all the time, he was the most troublesome. I decided to put Rum into his feed and I got a good nights sleep! For a time I used the Rum to ensure some peace but the family found out, you can imagine the beating I received. I had just one friend, I wasn't allowed out to play, I just continued to carry errands and do house work while I looked after the boys. My dad didn't attempt to help me or my sister out but I bided my time.

After I left school I was asked what I wanted to do, I told them that I just wanted to get married. My idea of marriage was doing what you wanted without asking permission and having friends. No sooner had I mentioned marriage then one was arranged. I was fifteen when I became engaged and sixteen when I married on August 6th 1949 and it was straight out of the frying pan and into the fire! Firstly, having worked so hard for my foster family, you would have thought that they would have paid for my wedding photos, they didn't and to this day I have no idea what I looked like as a bride.

After her marriage Adelaide left the city and went to live in the country miles from her family, her youngest sister remained with the foster parents and was treated better. Adelaide's foster parents moved away and she lost contact with her sister and her brothers. The fairy tale marriage that Adelaide had envisaged never happened:

Adelaide and Sir Jimmy Saville

"I gave birth to my first child when I was seventeen years old, the baby boy was premature and only lived for seven days. My second child, a girl was born when I was eighteen, two years later my third baby came along, another two years passed and I had a fourth child a boy, he died at the age of four and a half years. My baby boy was one month old when he died from scalded milk. By this time my brother in law had arrived in Britain, my husband joined him in the following year. After a year my husband sent for us and we arrived in London in August 1962, we lived in London for six months. In February 1963 we arrived in Aylesbury and boy was it cold! We had snow, ice, frost and fog, you name it we had it! It took me a long time to get over it, my youngest was born December fifth of that year, still births and other things happened. I applied for a job at Stoke Mandeville Hospital as a nursing auxiliary, I started work there in July 1965, I did this for five years. My marriage was falling apart and I couldn't cope with being disciplined, I had had enough of it. When my eldest was eighteen years old I applied to start my training as a nurse, it was a struggle but I kept going. Many times the electricity was cut off but myself and the children kept on studying. I got a lot of abuse from my husband (verbal most of the time) many times I was admitted as a patient with all sorts of problems. I completed my training in 1973, I won a prize for effort and it was presented to me by Sir Jimmy Saville. I was in charge of running the Rheumatology Ward at Stoke Mandeville until I retired. It was a pleasure nursing my patients, they were exceptionally kind and considerate, I enjoyed my nursing days, we worked as a team".

John Pilgrim interviews Adelaide for the 'Out and About' Radio Program

Adelaide's marriage came to an end in 1975 and in 1985 she applied to purchase the home she and her family lived in, they have never looked back and Adelaide is a proud house owner. Adelaide has suffered ill health throughout her working life but she never let anything get her down as she says: "There are many ways of choking a dog without putting a rope round its neck".

I thank Adelaide for allowing me the privilege of telling her story, there are many unsung heroes and heroines in this world and Adelaide Johnson is one of them.

Adelaide shows JP her magnificent garden

MK, (BC)

L ove it or hate it, everyone has their own view of Milton Keynes, from the concrete cows to the ski slope, from the lakes to the grand new theatre everyone has an opinion. I'm told that if you live in MK then you will be sure to wear out the tyres on your car quicker than anywhere else in Britain! What do you mean RUBBISH! It's true I tell you. Think about it for a minute, there must be more roundabouts in MK than anywhere else, or at least it seems like it, and the more corners you take, the more tyres you wear out.

They shot a lot of the sequences for the 'Superman' movie in Milton Keynes, they shot some near Eaton Bray as well as it happens, I know because a couple of the regulars in my pub worked as extras. They tell me that Gene Hackman is a 'good bloke' and plays a mean game of Poker! Anyway, back to Milton Keynes (If I must), I like it but I still get lost and don't care what anyone says, it is difficult to navigate. Things would have been much easier around 2000 B.C. when man first settled in the area (and they call MK a 'New Town'?). They lived close to the river and led simple lives raising cattle and growing crops. The earliest known house in the area is dated to around 700 B.C. (It has probably been extended a few times since and no doubt a conservatory has been added!). In case you are interested the house was found in the Blue Bridge area of Wolverton.

Milton Keynes Parish Church in the old village

The Romans visited the area as well and Watling Street is now roughly on the A4, they built a road from Fenny Stratford to Buckingham. The Romans also created Magiovinium, with a population of around fifteen hundred souls, other settlements were at Woughton, Wymbush and Stantonbury. Saxon sites have been found near Bradwell, Great Linford and Shenley Brook End, a gold brooch was found on a burial site at Shenley (rumours that this belonged to Ernie Almond are spurious).

So throughout history people inhabited the area now known as Milton Keynes (and probably got lost on the way). The site of the earliest dated windmill in this country was excavated at Great Linford and Bletchley Park would have seen the hunters tracking game in the many parks created by wealthy landowners in days gone by. AND STILL NOBODY SAW FIT TO BUILD SOME CONCRETE (or even wattle and daub) COWS!

The people of Newport Pagnall built a canal to link with the Grand Junction Canal in 1817 and the canal runs through the new city to this day. The railways came to MK and by 1838 the coaching trade was all but finished. Wolverton became the place where engines were changed and the expansion of the railway provided work. We won't go into the reasons as to why the area now known as Milton Keynes was chosen as the site for a *'New City'* nor will we discuss the virtues (or otherwise) of MK, suffice to say it is there, it is growing, it is vital and will not be ignored!

'Bob from Bletchley' tells me

It's the most important element of the radio programme, when people send me information about the places we cover. Bob wrote from Bletchley to advise me that a visit to the 'Cathedral in the Fields' would be worthwhile.

All Saints Church at Hillesden

The village of Hillesden is but a few short miles from Milton Keynes and is mentioned in the Domesday Book. The land, or a large amount of it was owned by a certain Hugh de Bolebec and was made of - *'pasture for fourteen ploughs and woodland to feed one hundred hogs all at the value of six pounds'*.

There was a church at Hillesden in the reign of Henry II, today's church dates from 1493. With the original Hillesden House, All Saints Church was part of a fortified outpost of the Royalist Forces of Charles II during the Civil War. It was besieged twice by the Parliamentary Forces in 1643, Oliver Cromwell took part in the second siege and Musket Ball holes can still be seen to this day. Some one hundred and forty Royalist prisoners, some of them were killed and buried in a nearby field. Hillesden House was burnt and Sir Alexander Denton, the Royalist commander was forced to watch this act, it is said that he died of a broken heart in 1645 and was buried at Hillesden.

All Saints Church is a Grade 1 listed building and, as is fairly common these days, a small hardworking band of volunteers is responsible for its care and maintenance.

IT'S ENOUGH TO DRIVE YOU QUACKERS!

They bred the famous Aylesbury ducks at Weston Turville, it was one of the main occupations in the village in the early part of the last century. I am told that the village had several ponds, not surprising really, the ducks had to have a swim didn't they? In the church of St Mary you can read the following:

The Widow Turpin's Gift

She gave all her freehold, leasehold, arable land and lay ground lying and being within the Parish and Common fields of Weston in the County of Bucks with all Commons and Profit there into belonging to Mary Hockley, for the term of her natural life and no longer and if she hath any children lawfully begotten on her Body, then they too have her land and lay ground aforesaid equally divided betwixt them and for want of such issue then immediately after her decease. She gave all the aforesaid estate to the 'Poor of Weston' aforesaid for ever: and that the overseers of the Poor of the said Parish of Weston and their successors shall at the best rate and for the most profit they can, let all be said estate and rents of the same shall be laid out only two shillings for their trouble in great loaves of good and wholesome bread to be equally distributed by them to the poorest inhabitants of the aforesaid Parish by equal portions on the feast of St Michael the Arch Angel and the Annunciation of the Blessed Virgin Mary.

The gift became due in the year 1736. Tokens for bread and flour are given to a number of elderly widows.

Aylesbury Ducks

From Espana to Bletchley - Roy's Story

Roy is a regular listener to the radio station and he often calls in, one day he related a story that, at the time was hard to believe. In 1997 Roy was working as a freelance translator and courier in Spain.

Roy's Story

"On the 8th of August 1997 I was drinking with some people in a bar in Torreviera, Spain near where I lived, I left the bar and took a taxi home arriving at around one a.m. on Saturday morning. On the 9th of August I was waiting for a bus, I had to go and buy a ticket for a flight to the UK. I was travelling to England to care for my 92 year old mother while my brother went on holiday. An unmarked car pulled up at the bus stop and I was asked if my name was Roy, when I replied that it was I was told that I was being arrested, I was bundled into the back of the car and handcuffed. At the police station I was asked to make a statement and they wanted to know if I knew someone named Thomas Jones, I told them that I didn't. It turned out that one of the men I had been drinking with the night before was called Thomas Jones, there were six people present at the interview and I was informed that one of them was a lawyer, though I couldn't tell you which one because he never spoke. I was informed that the police knew who had murdered Thomas Jones, they told me that if I named names I would be allowed to go, I couldn't tell the police anything because I didn't know anything.

Roy was taken to a very small room with no windows, no light or toilet facilities. He was given a bread roll and a bottle of water, sometime later he was taken to have his photograph taken.. The following day (Sunday) Roy was taken (at 2 am in the morning) to Gauradmar G.C. Station, he was given another bottle of water and a smoked salmon sandwich. At 10 am he was moved to the cells in the local court. Roy remained in the cell until Monday morning when he was taken to the court and accused of the murder of the man he had known as 'Steve', he agreed to a D.N.A. test safe in the knowledge that this would prove his innocence. You might feel that Roy had been through some sort of nightmare but this was only the beginning.

"Having been charged in court I was refused bail and returned to the cells, I was not allowed a razor to shave or toothpaste or soap. On Tuesday morning the police took me to my flat where a search was carried out, the police found nothing. I then went for the D.N.A. test on Wednesday, still I was refused washing facilities and so I refused to eat, I was seen by a doctor who declared that I had no health problems, I had my fingerprints taken and allowed to shave with cold water.

On the 23rd of August I was moved to another prison and placed in a cell with two others, we had to share a toilet and wash basin. At this time I was allowed to make my first telephone call to the British Consulate and a lawyer was found for me. As events turned out, I lost all track of time and after about six months I appeared in court to make a second application to be bailed, I was refused because the D.N.A results had not been sent to the court. Three months went by and still the results were not available, my lawyer became very irate and requested another court date or for me to be bailed, we were refused and then told that the judge handling the case had retired!

After two years in jail and several court appearances Roy appeared before another judge and was remanded in custody for a further two years. The D.N.A results finally came through, they indicated that Roy was in the clear, that was in August 1999. A new court date was set for October but in September someone found out that the judge was, yes you guessed it! RETIRING. On the 23rd of January 2000 Roy was found not guilty, he was released on the 27th of January. Outside the prison with no money Roy telephoned a friend, he now lives in Bletchley, Milton Keynes and is trying to put his life back together.

Others have been apprehended and found guilty of the crime Roy was accused of. It is impossible to believe what it must have been like for a man to be picked up off the street and incarcerated in a foreign jail, seemingly without any real hope and totally frustrated but thankfully Roy is here to tell the tale.

Dog Fights and Heroes - Dawn's Story

Dawn in Rushden, Northants has worked very hard to trace her family history. We have e-mailed each other, written to each other and telephoned each other and I am always impressed with Dawn's enthusiasm so I asked her to produce a short account of the experiences of her Great Grandpa Billy:

'My Great Grandpa was a remarkable man. Born William Herbert Harrison on the 4th of March 1889 in Marsh More, Hertfordshire, he was one of the pioneers of the Royal Flying Corps. Billy joined the Royal Engineers in January 1911, was posted to the Air Battalion in December 1911 and transferred to the RFC -on formation- in May 1912. In April 1915 he was posted to No 13 Squadron and on October 9th was sent to the Great War in France. Billy left a war diary from 1915, written in pencil and rather faded, but I sat enthralled as I read it and re-lived the agony, excitement and sadness that he experienced over The 'Somme' eighty five years ago'.

Extracts From Billy's Diary

October 19th - Machines arrived from England at about 12 noon or a little after. Bomb racks and Lewis guns fitted.

October 29th - Big meeting of Foreign Officers, may fly with one. Took on board ten one hundred pound bombs - having happy times with them.

November 8th - Went up at 6.30 am. with Lt. Porter to test air, found it rather cloudy so waited until later. At 9.50 went up again as gunner in BE2c 4092 as escort for bomb dropping at Bapaume. Crossed the firing line about 10.00 then had the first experience of 'Archie', but were too high for them at nine thousand feet. Came back over line at 10.55 after good exciting time. Wonderful panorama of clouds, landed at 11.15 quite excellent time.

November 26th - Rather cloudy but went as gunner to Mr O'Malley over Cambrai, coming back near Albert saw Hun at about five thousand feet. Dived from eleven thousand to five thousand, attacked him and drove him down. Believe the pilot killed and engine damaged. Hurrah! first blood to 'B' Flight 13 Squadron. I am quite the hero of the hour.

November 28th - Special mission early, then gunner to Mr O'Malley in 4070 over Cambrai and Bapaume, bitter cold, had only crossed lines when he saw machine above us. Went on nearly to Bapaume then were attacked by Fokker monoplane. Flying wire cut, rear spar nearly shot away. My gun jammed and I could do nothing. Returned quite all right.

November 30th - Special Mission, early morning. Afternoon with Lt. Porter chased machine east of Amiens but lost in clouds. Above clouds for about forty five minutes then found ourselves over Hebuterne, then went on to Arras and saw marvellous sight a network of trenches and 'Archies'. Got well shelled but no hits. Picked out 'Archie' battery.

December 5th - Observer with Captain Knight to Nesle, he got wind up and nearly did it. I thought he was going to land over enemy territory. Don't want to go up with him again.

January 23rd - Better weather. Some flying but not for me. Never mind though, have had my share and now roll on 'Blighty' for a few days. Could do with a pleasant change.

First World War diary from 1915 belonging to William Harrison (My Great Grandpa Billy)

The back page of the diary contains Great Grandpa Billy's *"last message"* to his wife Lillian and three year old son Graham just in case he didn't make it back from the war. I cannot read it without getting a lump in my throat.

"To my wife,

If I should fall in this most strenuous of wars, you will know that I died an honourable death fighting for my King and Country and my wife and child. I admit that I need never have flown over the German lines if I had not wished it, but as I am not by any means a coward, I wished to do my share in the actual

fighting. I won my first honour on Friday November twenty sixth by bringing down a German machine and on Sunday I very nearly got brought down with my pilot owing to my gun jamming in the air. As you may see I have been over the German territory many times and I think I can safely say I have done my best in every way for the glorious Mother Country - Old England. I trust that everything I have here will be sent to you and that you will always remember your soldier husband.

Be true to his trust and wishes always. May God bless and protect you and my darling Sonny ever more.

From your loving husband Will"

Thankfully Great Grandpa made it home and served in the RFC and RAF until April 1935 when he retired, however when World War Two broke out he was recalled to service.

Great Grandpa Billy Harrison

This 1940 photograph shows both Great Grandpa Billy and his son (my Grandfather) Graham William Harrison. Graham was Chief Flying Instructor for Melling Aviation in Kent and a RAF Volunteer Reserve from 1935. He was called up in 1939 for the duration of the hostilities. Graham was a RAF Flying Instructor and was later posted to 235 Squadron where he flew many Strike Wing operations with Coastal Command.

On the twentieth of April 1944 his squadron were flying an Offensive Patrol in formation over the Bay of Biscay, flying at an average height of two hundred feet, although at times as low as fifty feet. At 14.13 hrs. pilots Jimmie Rodgers and Ted Armstrong saw Flight Lt. Harrison's ageing Beaufighter appear to hit a down draught. The plane dropped with the port propeller striking the sea and tearing off. The engine caught fire and after wrestling with the plane for two minutes they were forced to ditch into the sea.

Although he and his navigator, Flight Lt. Adrian Evan Jones got out of the aircraft before it sank (in just twenty seconds according to other planes flying with them), they never managed to get into the aircraft dinghy as the wind and currents blew it away from them. The other members of the squadron were completely helpless as they circled overhead literally watching the boys drown. Grandpa Billy was re-retired in 1944 and lived to be 98 years old. He never really got over the loss of his only son who is listed on the War Memorial in North Berwick, Scotland and in the book of remembrance in Edinburgh castle.

Dawn of Rushden

I am so very proud of Great Grandpa Billy and Grandpa Graham, they were brave men, my heroes and this is my tribute to them.

'ARCHIES'

Grandpa Billy's reference to 'Archies' caused some discussion on the radio programme and it was 'Dave the Thatcher' from Milton Keynes who put us right:

It seems that in the early days of World War I the British paid little attention to German inventions and indeed were prone to make 'somewhat eccentric' jokes about them. One such invention was the anti-aircraft gun and the objects it fired (AA), the word 'Archie' is believed to have come from a popular music hall song of the time sung by George Robey, "Archibald certainly not" were the key words of the song. The French appeared to have taken anti-aircraft guns more seriously and invented their own version, the British soon followed. By the end of the Great War the Germans were said to have possessed around two thousand five hundred and seventy six such guns, there were three hundred and sixty four with the British Army in France. British pilots training in England were told little or nothing about 'Archie', being much too busy coping with the day to day hazards of ordinary flying. I have been told from other sources that the areas mentioned in 'Grandpa Billy's' diary were particularly heavily inhabited by 'Archie'.

Thatching in the area of Little Gaddesden, Herts circa 1912

AND SPEAKING OF DAVE THE THATCHER

Dried reed stems have been used for thousands of years as thatching as well as for basketry, arrows, pens and in musical instruments. King Edward II (1307 - 27) is said to have enjoyed thatching, he also enjoyed ditch digging, swimming and theatricals. Edward's reign is considered by historians to have been rather less than successful; he had a close friend named Piers Gaveston who had been exiled by Edward's father because of the friendship. When '*Ed the two*' came to the throne he brought back Piers and continued his close relationship (as well as ditch digging and thatching of course). We will now move on a few hundred years and get to the point.

Dave the Thatcher working in the village of Flitton, 2000

DAVE SAYS

"*I was born on 8th June, 1955, the midwife missed her breakfast and I was born at my grandparents house in Dunstable rather than at home. My first school was in Chiltern Road, the building now houses a radio station that I don't listen too! After my first day at school I decided that I wanted to retire, my grandad had recently retired as Headmaster of Northfield School and I wanted to join him! I failed my eleven plus exams, I have never been any good at exams or writing but I was good at history and loved going to museums. While I was at Northfield's it wasn't too bad because they knew my grandad had been Headmaster and I got away with a few things. I really loved aeroplanes as my Grandmother had worked at Handley Page; I joined the Air Training Corps and wanted to go into the Royal Airforce. When I was fourteen my dad took me along to a recruiting office, they told me that I would hear from them but I never did. I hated my last two years at school and became a bit of a rebel, I even considered running away to Wales!*

One day my mum was listening to Woman's Hour on the radio and she heard someone talking about thatching, she suggested that I should try it. The speaker was a man named Fred Cooper from Knuston Hall. We got his address from the BBC and Fred came to visit me at our home in Dunstable. After a while I went to work part time with Haig and Tomkins at Willington, they told me to get some qualifications, so it was back to school! I managed to achieve a GCE in Technical Drawing. My dad bought me a motorbike when I was sixteen, motorbikes played a big part in my life for the next twelve years. I finally managed to gain an apprenticeship with Dodson Thatching Services, I did three years and then another two as an Improver. After five years living in digs, eating fish paste sandwiches, I gave up, I still can't stand fishpaste! I moved back to Dunstable and got a job at Vauxhall's in the paint shop. I hated every minute of the day, they kept telling me to slow down. I finally went to see Frank Purser in Toddington, he rang around and secured a job for me working on my own, since that time I have been a self- employed Thatcher, it's a good job, the weather is bad at times but I like it".

Radio Producer Nigel Gayler steadies a nervous Pilgrim, while Dave looks on!

This book is dedicated to my wife Margaret,
daughters: Sarah, Emma and Johanna
who support me always and to my
grandchildren Sam, Joe and Emily
and their dad, Michael.

Spainy displays his love of giraffes, Pilgrim shows his love for Spainy and Nick disassociates himself!

JOIN JOHN ON THE WEB!

It's up and running and you can be part of it. Find out more about your town or village, what used to happen and what's happening now. See pictures taken from David Spain's extensive archive and talk to John. There's a weekly column written by John Pilgrim. Family history, gardening, wartime memories, celebrity interviews, book reviews and much more. If it's about people, places and their passions we want to include it. You are invited to take part.

www.outandabout.uk.net

Also by John Pilgrim:
Out & About Book I
(published 1999)

BIBLIOGRAPHY

THE STORY OF THE JAYWICK SANDS ESTATE - MARY LYONS - PHILLIMORES   ISBN 9 781860 770128

SUFFOLK /JOHN BURKE /B.T. BATSFORD /   ISBN 0 7134 0069 2

SCOTT'S GROTTO - DAVID PERMAN - THE WARE SOCIETY   ISBN 09509259 2 6

A PICTORIAL GUIDE TO ROYSTON CAVE - P.T.HOULDCROFT   ISBN D-9511722 5 5
ROYSTON LOCAL HISTORY SOCIETY

BIGGLES! - PETER BERRESFORD ELLIS AND JENNIFER SCHOFIELD   ISBN 1-874105-26-X
VELOCE PUBLISHING

A HERTFORDSHIRE VALLEY - SCOTT HASTIE AND DAVID SPAIN   ISBN 0-9528631-0-3
ALPINE PRESS

CORAM'S CHILDREN - CHRISTINE OLIVER AND PETER AGGLETON   ISBN 0-9536613 - 1- 8
CORAM FAMILY

BEDFORDSHIRE - JAMES DYER - SHIRE COUNTY GUIDES   ISBN 0-7478-0269-6

THE BEDFORDSHIRE VILLAGE BOOK - BEDFORDSHIRE WI   ISBN 1-853060143
COUNTRYSIDE BOOKS

LEAFLETS AND INFORMATION GUIDES FROM VARIOUS COUNTIES

PLEASE NOTE: WHERE I HAVE QUOTED TELEPHONE NUMBERS AND OPENING TIMES, THEY ARE CORRECT AT THE TIME OF PRINTING. IF YOU HAVE ANY DIFFICULTIES PLEASE CHECK YOUR TELEPHONE BOOK AND DON'T RING ME!